8 Dynamic Weapons for Conquering Life's Illusions

Robert Meyer

Copyright © 2015 by Robert Meyer
All Rights Reserved. This book or any portion thereof may not be reproduced or used in any manner whatsoever without the express written permission of the publisher except for the use of brief quotations in a book review.

Printed in the United States of America

First Printing, 2015

ISBN-13: 978-1519299321
ISBN-10: 151929932X

Dedicated to all those wonderful teachers who supplied me with the Dynamic Weapons that helped me conquer my illusions.

Table of Contents

Introduction: Conquering Life's Illusions..1

Chapter One: Dynamic Anti-Social Altruism Weapon............................5

Chapter Two: Dynamic Anti-Irrational Selfishness Weapon...............13

Chapter Three: Dynamic Rational Selfishness Weapon......................35

Chapter Four: Dynamic Unhampered Capitalism Weapon.................47

Chapter Five: Dynamic Mind Power Weapon.......................................73

Chapter Six: Your Dynamic Weapons – A Daily Affair.........................93

Chapter Seven: Dynamic Accelerated Awareness Weapon..............117

Chapter Eight: Dynamic Joy of Existence Weapon............................149

Chapter Nine: Dynamic Strategic Action Weapon.............................173

Chapter Ten: Dynamic Secret Weapon and Beyond.........................195

Special thanks to Tyler Dylan Brown who supplied his brilliance along with an abundance of written research material. Without his input this book would not have been possible.

How does a man or woman conquer life's illusions and experience the joy of his or her existence when everything seems chaotic?

INTRODUCTION

CONQUERING LIFE'S ILLUSIONS

Of all the threats that face us in modern society there exists a fear so deep that it's uncertain if it can ever be shaken. The modern era has been marked by continuous boom and bust cycles, devastating Main Street, and awarding the politically connected on Wall Street. We have been in the midst of a recession that was actually a depression and then in a recovery that looks likes a recession. Year after year of poor government policy and massive government interventionism in our lives created an instability that permeates the market place. Deficit spending, zero interest rate policies, the drug war, the war on poverty, military excursions and other large centrally managed government schemes devalue everything they touch. Additional violations of personal liberty, economic freedom and individual rights left our nation in a state of disarray. Not only that but they have severely strained the back of the legitimate economy that has carried them. Atlas is beginning to shrug. Massive bailouts, nightmare levels of Quantitative Easing (QE) along with the multi-trillion dollar secret Paulson bailout severely decreased the local and global purchasing power parity of the US Dollar. With the destruction of the American Way of Life and the American Dream, what should an individual do? How does a man or woman conquer life's illusions and experience the joy of his or her existence when everything seems chaotic?

As incredible as it might seem to you, generations of Americans believed the illusion that government can control the economy, making their lives easier and more prosperous. Historical evidence to the contrary in form of the ruins of empires strewn across the earth proves that illusions die hard. An entire nation (the USSR) that rivaled the United States had a massive centralized economy with the greatest assortment of wealth and resources on this planet. We all know how that one turned out. Isn't it obvious that a centralized economy in Russia or Germany failed miserably? Why do people think American exceptionalism applies in this blanket statement. Of course, the establishment has done everything possible to reinforce the illusion that we need the Government in order to keep us equal. Conquering illusions means we realize that instead of equality we get the systematic oppression of the population with a worse distribution of wealth than South Africa under Apartheid. Incredibly, we're told that we need more and more regulations to protect the economy and the American Dream. We're spoon fed the lies that we could not access the American Dream if it weren't for the saintly American Government.

In a nation founded on State's rights, the United States has gone far beyond Federalist and is now a City-State that rules over the rest of the nation. Obviously, politicians and bureaucrats made sure the citizens of our once great nation became dependent on the government for their very existence, reducing them to government benefit addicts.

Generation X - the generation that could have changed it all - was successfully subverted by consumerism, vulture capitalism, which is actually anti-capitalism, and fell victim to the good old "divide and conquer" strategy, Sadly, they didn't even realize it. The establishment media strengthens the illusion that a vast government machinery is needed to protect the American Dream. Of course, the mainstream media pumps out vast propaganda, hitting every media stream available. Their devilish influence stretches across oceans, manipulating google search result pages, spawning fake social media accounts and phony PSA's by celebrities paid vast sums to say a 10 second phrase. From a business perspective who wouldn't do that?

Once people refuse to give up their illusions, they become dangerously attached to floating abstractions that mutate into delusions that destroy everything America once stood for. The American Dream has become corrupted and idealized in a fantastic fairy tale. Establishment teachers indoctrinate the precious minds of children with propaganda, lies and half-truths.

Now it's time to conquer the first illusion, one that personally and socially causes much damage. In ways it is very similar to a cult or cult-like religion. Nobody wants to admit that their deeply held beliefs, ones they accumulated and planned their existence around are blatantly false. Even though the discovery can be devastating, hope awaits you with open arms. You will soon realize that believing illusions and myths can be destructive to your well-being. Conquering their evil ways forever empowers you.

How do you use your Dynamic Anti-Social Altruism Weapon? You give up the role of a victim, become a warrior for personal liberty and economic freedom. The result. You not only survive, but you also thrive.

CHAPTER ONE

DYNAMIC ANTI-SOCIAL ALTRUISM WEAPON

For a thought experiment I want you to consider the following: Social Altruism masquerades as a caring philosophy of selflessness and self-sacrifice. In addition, Social Altruists claim they are loving and giving and so is the philosophy they base their life around. Guess what? You just discovered an illusion. The reality of the matter is that Social Altruism exists as a cannibalistic philosophy of hate and plunder. It has been subverted and institutionalized by Governments as a means to confiscate the wealth of productive citizens. Few greater crimes are committed than those in the name of the common good. Avaricious politicians have resorted to it despite the fact that its malicious manifestation could destroy America systematically from the inside-out. For these reasons I surmise and believe that Social Altruism reigns over us as the philosophy of anti-life. In order to conquer it, you need a weapon of attack and self-defense. I am pleased to offer you the Dynamic Anti-Social Altruism Weapon. Let's supply you plenty of ammo.

The Liberal Media portrays and pitches Social Altruism as the way to solve all of our problems. These purveyors of injustice change the term to "social justice" and attempt to play your emotions of shame and guilt rather than reason, logic and objective law. The Social Altruist easily stomps on individual rights, your rights.

How can anyone claim he or she exists a loving being when their social policies violate the rights of others on institutionalized levels. Despite violence being at modern historical lows, Social Altruists, do-gooders and world-improvers feed us stories of shootings and outlying cases of violence. Of course, we are told that we suffer from an epidemic of violence—and guns are the cause of the problem. In addition, you can expect Social Altruists to attempt to disarm you of your intellectual and psychological weapons. That's what the politically correct BS is all about. Be sure to have your Dynamic Anti-Social Altruism Weapon ready at all times.

The would be dictators hide the sorry fact that it's their social policies that make people poor and desperate. To cover up their misdeeds the Social Altruist blames the gun. Yeah, the gun commits the crime.

Ask any Social Altruist to look at California and the decay of the once great state to see how some of their policies turned out long term. It's fun being a member of the good idea club: especially when you don't have to pay for any of your "experiments." People are kept in fear because fear is effective and fear is the primary tool Social Altruists use, with the emotion of envy running a close second. How can you trust news sources that promiscuously sleep with the government and its cronies. The screwing begins once members of the elite and their mouthpieces begin manipulating your emotions and exploiting your deepest and darkest fears.

Here's something you should never forget. Social Altruism not only destroys the ones providing the help but also the ones receiving the help as well. The people on the bottom, the ones "helped", we can refer to as the plundered. These unfortunate individuals suffer lower participation in labor markets, diminished productivity, and end up living in a society dependent on foreign/government help. You can see that people cornered in a suffocating existence become mired in hopelessness. On the other hand, the bold, independent person sees his earned rewards diminishing. How about the plundering of the productive middle class. You don't want to see your lifestyle reduced to nothing but the nourishment of your basic needs. It's time to Ready, Aim, Fire.

Government and the Social Altruist

Let's supply the example of government provided housing. Bureaucrats (Social Altruists) keep their tenants on a very short leash—and in many cases can arbitrarily boot people from their homes. From this you can surmise that all kinds of nasty things can be done to keep people in compliance. Can you imagine these government directives advancing into the lives of the mainstream? Well, I have to news for you. It's already happening on a rapid basis. Don't you wish the government would just leave you alone. Can you see why it's necessary for you to conquer life's illusions ASAP. You must effectively use your Anti-Social

Altruism Weapon.

In the end, total social productivity, savings and investment all plummet, setting the nation back years. One example I'd like to turn to is Cuba. Despite their socialistic inefficiencies and years of suffering from sanctions, embargoes and blockades, its people have created a self sufficient economy and medical system. Adversity forced them to be as efficient as possible simply because of resource limitations. Had the US been giving them foreign aid (which usually ends up a complete disaster) instead of quarantining them, the outcome of Cuba would have been more similar to Haiti or the Dominican Republic than to a capitally dry Singapore in the Caribbean. Of course, communism kept Cuba in a dismal state of unsatisfied desire.

We will continue to use our Anti-Social Altruism Weapon to conquer the Social Altruism illusion with the following bit of wisdom. When resources are not earned or honestly acquired, no incentive exists for technological advancements. The result: Bad ideas born of illusion create dependent societies and cultures that stall out once the government unwittingly flicks the reversal switch.

Despite all of this you can still enjoy your existence. You can learn to live life as a free and happy individual, protected by individual rights versus the mob rule of American democracy. It's important to know where you stand as an individual in order to see the dark path that most members of society ignorantly stumble down. Yes, you can live happily within the constraints presented. The first thing you can do is to stop supporting the predatory philosophy that Social Altruism dumps on people. Plain and simple, Social Altruists present an anti-life philosophy that unfortunately permeates society.

Did you know that Adolph Hitler was a moralist? He lived his brutal life as a Social Altruist, finally mutating in a Social Nihilist. He rose to success working in Public Health. Gee, it's too bad we don't have him around as a member of the ObamaCare team. Anyway, his many policy "successes" included banning pregnant women from smoking or drinking, levying fines on businesses that were caught selling alcohol or tobacco products and even going after hard drugs like Cocaine, drugs that had made their way into Europe from South America.

As soon as we surrender to the Government and allow them to set policy with "evidence based practices" the problem manifests on the macro scale. That guarantees hurting more people than are helped. A Social Altruist sees a couple of hundred people per every 100,000 as an acceptable loss, even when humanism and individualism scream out the contrary. Acceptable losses apply to the potatoes you had to move 600 miles to throw in a big stew. Some will rot and some will fall off the truck, but we don't stop the entire truck on the highway to pick up one potato that fell off and the potatoes that have rotted will simply be thrown away without any other thought. The takeaway is that Men and Women are not potatoes and should not be thought of as acceptable losses that advance policies in the name of overall good. How can a society claim to represent the needs of all when it trivializes the rights of quite a few?

You need to face the fact that the Social Altruist cares nothing for the individual or his loved ones. He cares nothing for you. People are just sacrificial fodder for his demented social schemes. Now you see why you need a Dynamic Weapon of self defense.

The establishment, the incumbents, the banks and the Federal Government would like you to just keep plowing forward—trying to reach the dragon that masquerades as the American Dream. Of course, these power players play a rigged game that guarantees you never get to the final level. The idea and motto towards the American Public by elitists is that "they must be kept dumb." These purveyors of human misery and degradation consider you a tool of exploitation. They attempt to acquire your continued support by the large scale victimization of innocent people. Incredibly their pandering ways garner large scale support.

Conquering life's illusions means that you successfully stand up for your personal liberty and economic freedom, even though the Social Altruist's politically correct nonsense seems to make it more admirable to play the part of a victim. Isn't it sickening that society's liberty violators label you as troublemaker instead of a potential leader when you make a positive stand for your individual rights? Our Founding Fathers would probably be jailed as terrorists. Now here are men who knew how to use their weapons.

You realize that doing the right thing isn't easy, and the easy things to do are seldom right. In order to move forward you need to withdraw your support from this emotionally manipulative system and discover your personal power. Of course, the Anti-Social Altruism Weapon supplies you a considerable amount of power.

How do you use your Dynamic Weapon? You give up the role of a victim, become a warrior for personal liberty and economic freedom. The result. You not only survive, but you also thrive. I believe we successfully conquered the Social Altruism illusion.

Personal Altruism

At this point in time you may be wondering about the role of voluntarily helping others. Shouldn't our some of our goals include helping the less fortunate, family members and close friends? Such scenarios are hardly cut and dry and I can pull from my personal experiences to attest to that fact.

Imagine that your life has presented you with the situation that finds one of your friends, relatives or for the sake of an exercise an acquaintance in a dire situation. As humans, we are thinking, sensing, feeling creatures. You know that it's hard not to feel some emotion and empathy when you're dealing with fellow men and women. Your heart goes out to them because they're people you truly care about or trust. It is almost impossible to ignore their difficulties, and if it is your own child or parent that is experiencing problems it is virtually impossible to turn them down.

For your own well-being and safety, you must acknowledge the fact that humans are especially emotional and fickle characters. We make terrible decisions under stress and we often act like irrational investors in our personal and financial affairs. Are you beginning to feel that monkeys throwing darts at a board of goals could allocate your capital and time better than all the elite planning and trading schemes you dream up?

You might wonder what the heck is going on. What happens is that we allow our heartfelt emotions to take over because it feels right. We send our head on a permanent vacation. Here's a situation where you can become your own worst enemy. You unwittingly take the role of a

Social Altruist. You don't want your Dynamic Weapon used against you.

You begin conquering your illusions when you become a thinker instead of an automatic response mechanism. Emotions can offer you wonderful feelings and experiences. Unfortunately, your feelings might convince you to move ahead with your decision, despite the fact that you must sacrifice your valuable time and money. There's an old saying that the road to hell is paved with good intentions. You think it's possible that it could apply to some of your altruistic endeavors?

When someone you trust or care about is in trouble you feel the same pain they feel, despite not being in direct affliction of it. That's called empathy. Tragically, more often than not the person you helped ends up worse off. He or she fails to help themselves, ending up much weaker. In the process this unfortunate person loses his initiative, drive, responsibility, perception of self and sense of self reliance.

As mentioned earlier, the person you helped isn't the only party who was negatively affected by the altruistic blunder. You have to face the unhappy fact that you ended up losing. Your time and (or) your money vanished. You definitely want to trade value for value. A negative value for a negative value shouldn't be to your liking. To add insult to injury, you don't even get the satisfaction of a job well done. You sabotage your peace of mind by dwelling upon the possibility that if you hadn't interfered in the first place that person might be better off. Even worse, your sacrifice is not appreciated, and your trust with this individual has changed. Chances are you will enter future relationships with a fundamentally different attitude, maybe one of distrust. That's not the happy consequence you were hoping for. You allowed a tricky situation to disarm you.

I'm certainly not ashamed to admit this has happened to me several times. You would think I learned my lesson the first time, but instead I'm just like everyone else. A good adage that applies here is *"What you don't learn through wisdom you learn through woe."* It's a lot better to struggle gaining wisdom than to be captured by woe. I hope you can learn to do the same; minimize woe by maximizing your drive for wisdom.

Please don't get me wrong, I believe in helping people. Doing small favors for others is pleasurable, it builds trust and relationships and it increases your sense of community. You feel good helping your elderly neighbor plant a tree and she feels good because of the increased and deepened personal relationship you both developed. It's nice to have some allies.

What we just described about your neighbor isn't where the danger lurks. I would encourage you to help people out with little things that only need fixed once and are not chronologically or monetarily detrimental to your well-being. It builds the sense of community and brings everyone together. Plus he or she will be much more likely to do things for you in the future without being asked. When you don't have to ask someone for help because he easily and conveniently offers assistance, you don't have to deal with the differing expectations that form and eventually clash. Big favors like providing long term extended aid can fall into the dangerous category, but the danger is waived if it helps everyone involved. Otherwise your good intentions could be destructive to the one you're attempting to assist. We need to build people up. We definitely don't want to unwittingly break them down.

Conclusion

When there's extended economic hardship and market downturn you must be very careful to scrutinize and discriminate between truth and falsehood. You gain an expanded awareness when you see through the social and monetary illusions presented by the Federal Government, the Federal Reserve System, zombie corporations and people who support corrupt institutions. You must deal with your illusions sooner rather than later; otherwise they turn into epic delusions that collapse and crush you, demolishing your world view in the process.

You now possess a Dynamic Weapon with plenty of ammo to be used against Social Altruists who happen to cross your path. Isn't conquering life's illusions exciting? What do you say we move on to Dynamic Weapon #2.

The Anti-Irrational Selfishness Weapon is not only designed to protect you from others, but to also protect you from your own irrationally selfish impulses.

CHAPTER TWO

DYNAMIC ANTI-IRRATIONAL SELFISHNESS WEAPON

In the previous chapter, we discussed how detrimental the anti-life philosophy of Social Altruism is for your happiness and well-being. Irrational selfishness ties in with Social Altruism because Social Altruists need irrationally selfish people in order for their illusory social schemes to work.

Studies have shown that people who engage in pretentious diets, take part in excessive charity and philanthropy, adopt ineffective exercise programs and gravitate towards cult-like activities tend to be self-deluded. You must realize that quite often the compulsive seeker allows irrationally selfish behavior to control his thoughts and actions. He knows he needs to change, but because he's completely out of touch with reality, any fad or illusion captures his attention.

Social Altruism and irrational selfishness run hand in hand trying to achieve the same illogical goals that start as good intentions by people who have no knowledge of the situation. In other cases, self destructive actors behave in irrationally selfish ways, attracting the company of Social Altruists—that include the likes of world-improvers and do-gooder politicians. These purveyors of human misery find a cause to rally behind or some behavior they don't like to campaign against. Unfortunately it's dangerous to be an individual in today's society. You don't want to caught in an unfocused crossfire. Here's where you need both of your Dynamic Weapons, the Anti-Irrational Selfishness Weapon and the Anti-Social Altruism Weapon. Ready, Aim, Fire.

In the days of the Roaring Twenties and alcohol prohibition, the nation feasted on legends epitomized by the likes of the Great Gatsby, Babe Ruth, Charles Lindbergh and more. Unfortunately the artificial boom of the late 1920's comparable of the dot com boom of the late 1990's became the expectation of what is "normal." Our nation chasing boom and bust cycles that continually weaken us compares to a heroin addict trying to get a fix. The junkie needs more and more dope to get the same effect just as the Fed has to dose the economy with more and more fiat money to pump it up. Tragically, no amount of supply can do the job, resulting in the drug addict screaming in misery as he or she withdrawals from the lost ecstasy provided by the drug. You know, that sounds like the same "fix" the Federal Reserve find itself in. The drugs of Quantitative Easing (QE) and Zero Interest Rate Policy (ZIRP) barely stimulate the economy.

Tragically, quite a few unfortunate people destroy themselves with excessive alcohol consumption. Now we have the spectacle of it growing from a quiet personal matter to a matter of public health. Obviously, it's futile expecting health bureaucrats to solve the problem. Believing politicians and government bureaucrats can solve problems is an illusion you must conquer. Only you can solve your problems. That's why the Anti-Irrational Selfishness Weapon is not only designed to protect you from others, but to also protect you from your own irrationally selfish impulses.

To get to the root of irrational selfishness, we will use alcohol as an example. By the way we believe moderate consumption of alcohol to be both pleasurable and healthy. Self-control is the key to success.

Prohibition

Alcoholism is a personal problem exaggerated by psycho-social situations that provide little more than guaranteed oppression. The alcoholic behaves in ways that a normal person would not behave. Plain and simple, the lush over-indulges in the drink(s) of choice. Now that's what you call irrational selfishness. The Social Altruist waits at the end of the slippery slope to government interference. He sees this as an opening to form some sort of government campaign in order to save people from themselves. Reality tell us that some people will pursue the "pleasures" of alcohol, marijuana, cocaine, meth and heroin regardless of whether they're legal or illegal.

Discovering another social problem supplies the Social Altruist the drug he craves day after day. In his "ecstasy" he lobbies the government to completely re-regulate the market due to the tragic deaths of a few unfortunate souls. He appears oblivious to the fact that increasing government involvement does nothing to improve public safety. In fact, criminalization of drugs makes society a more dangerous place to live.

Back in the 1920's Congress banned alcohol with an amendment forbidding the sale of alcohol. You probably know the sorry results of that dangerous piece of legislation. Crooked government officials drove the price of alcohol way up, coordinated with criminal distribution gangs, and squashed any competition with violence or the threat of violence.

Let me ask you the following question. Should we go ahead and ban alcohol, cars, punish people who drink and drive, do nothing, exploit it, or learn from it? I opt that we learn from it. The Social Altruist only sees through the visors of the social agendas he pushes. Of course he has the involvement, blessing and financing of the elites, who desire to protect their territory and expand their reach. Darn, it sounds as if I'm describing government created drug cartels.

Maybe a simple public announcement/service campaign telling people the dangers of drinking and driving will be enough? Maybe better mental health services could completely solve the situation. These are solutions that target the individual—and tries to get him (her) to make the right choice on his own accord. Of course, we have to consider the fact that government solutions seldom achieve the desired results. You know by now that when a Social Altruist offers you help, it's Ready, Aim, Fire.

On the other side of the deal, Social Altruists loathe the individual and believe in a new order of rights that would turn America into the world's largest nanny-state. If these are outlying problems caused by lone individuals why must ineffective mass punishments and other blanketing regulations and limitations be imposed? Social Altruists don't understand the individual. These creators of massive social problems refuse to acknowledge the power of someone making the right choice on his own. It's impossible to fix problems caused by individuals en masse. It just doesn't work. We're not dealing with a high school hockey team, a block in County Jail or the Marines Corps boot camp. Unfortunately our government treats us like we still belong in nursery school. Maybe new gun control laws will permit toy guns. We have something more powerful than make-believe guns. We possess the

Dynamic Weapons of Anti-Social Altruism and Anti-Irrational Selfishness. Ready, Aim, Fire.

I really don't need to go into all the gory details about how prohibition, America's great social experiment crashed and burned. Prohibition quickly proved that not only could the government not regulate legal markets, but it also proved it completely inept at disrupting black markets that had sprung up around them. The war on alcohol ended the way the war on drugs should end.

Drinking alcohol is a victimless crime. It's firmly entrenched in the majority of the cultures world-wide. From Coconut & Pulp wines from the South Pacific, the Ancient Egyptians and modern European states all demonstrate drinking as a large facet of social involvement, culture and gatherings. When the government pushed the price of alcohol way up, it created a tremendous incentive to bring more of it to the domestic market. The government's ill-fated prohibition schemes resulted in the production of dangerous bathtub gin made with anti-freeze. Do you think it's likely that moralistic morons end up in charge of social affairs? You can count on government measures to worsen any situation.

To make matters worse, prohibition caused the alcohol trade to become so insanely profitable that organized crime sprung up around it. We ended up with the likes of Al Capone, an American gangster who led a crime syndicate dedicated to smuggling and bootlegging of liquor and other illegal activities during the Prohibition era. Talk about legends. The prohibition gangsters go down in history as household names, including the Kennedys, who got their start smuggling and selling moonshine. We can assume that it's a short step from the streets of crime to the political arena.

Rum running crafts would outrun the US Coast Guard to deliver alcohol to the shores to be smuggled rapidly into supply. These boats later formed the basis for the US Navy landing crafts used in the South Pacific, Africa and Europe. So in a way you can blame prohibition on giving us the Kennedys. Here's a family that captured the reputation of American Royalty. We're not sure why they deserve to be compared with Kings, Queens, Princes and Princesses. Still, the legend lives on.

Putting the proof in the pudding is the fact that despite widespread enforcement, people created independent underground networks in supply and distribution. It was called the Roaring 20's for a reason. As soon as the Amendment was repealed drinking rates actually dropped. Funny how the laws of supply and demand build up—then crush a black market instantly. Unfortunately, one of the favorite pastimes of members of the political and financial establishment remains tinkering with or denying universal laws. Your Dynamic Weapons protect you from people who deny reality.

The same economic laws that doomed prohibition are also the ones that spell doom for the drug war. It is admitted by virtually everyone that the government has no hope of winning the drug war. Independent studies conclude that propagandists and special interests falsified the data in order to impose the drug war on hapless citizens. Yeah, you've been lied to. It's becoming obvious that marijuana isn't even in the same league as the legal dangerous drugs that Big Pharma pushes on unsuspecting people.

Manufactured Evidence and the Social Altruist

Here's something that tells you not to trust establishment research. Volumes of research has been performed by nearly every federal agency as well as a multitude of universities. The fact that they were able to falsify data and get false peer-reviews shows exactly how we can't trust "evidence based systems." Social Altruists use manufactured evidence in order to hoodwink the masses in supporting a massive stomping on individual rights. Sometimes you need to Ready, Fire, Aim instead of the reliable Ready, Aim, Fire. These liberty-violators often ambush you.

You begin conquering life's illusions once you learn to break away from mass thinking. Your freedom resides in independent thinking. Now that's some powerful ammo.

The US government and US universities trivialized the entire scientific method and practice in order to push a non-scientific agenda. The Pharmaceutical companies just wanted to profit. Suppressing natural health methods in order to push questionable drugs seems to lack good moral substance. Social Altruists and establishment politicians believe that whatever they want to do is moral. They consider lying and stealing in the name of their social agendas perfectly acceptable behavior. Liars and cheats abolish the word "ethical" from their vocabulary.

It's time to call into question every single study the government has ever stamped with their approval. For your sake, you must realize that establishment institutions possess very little credibility. What's sad is the discovery that Social Altruists run the anti-philosophy department of the scientific community. These so-called do-gooders use their influence to tear down the name of Science in order to pursue their objectives. Who do they think they are...Emperor Chin?

Not only have we seen attacks on the scientific system and process but we've seen attacks on Economic Law—which have recently intensified in fear and aggression against all logic and reason. This is a big reason why we are witnesses to the continued economic problems our country faces. Modern economists deny Economic Law. That's similar to a physicist denying the laws of physics. Discovering that Economic Law is eternal goes a long way towards you conquering life's illusions.

Ok, let's move on.

What if major players in your life influence your thoughts, feelings and actions. It's important that you carefully choose the people you allow into your life. Who do you want to be a part of your precious existence? Who do you think should serve as building blocks in your life? If someone cannot support the basic rights of the individual (you're an individual, right) he or she should not be trusted under any circumstances whatsoever.

It's easier to conquer life's illusions when you keep good company and trusted allies.

We can conclude that just as you must shun the anti-life philosophy of altruism, you must rid all irrational selfishness from your life. It is also critical that you avoid the company of the irrationally selfish when possible.

Irrational Selfishness in Others

It's always interesting to note the old saying about keeping good company. Nearly all old-fashioned wisdom applies to the trials and tribulations of living in the modern day and the modern era. Some people think that we must do away with everything that is old, even things that work. You know, it's out with the old and in with the new. It's a bad joke to say that all of the old ways are inapplicable—a broad and bold generalization that would display one's true ignorance. You conquer illusions when you discover eternal wisdom. In fact, you supply your Dynamic Anti-Irrational Selfishness Weapon with the ammo of eternal wisdom.

The laws of human action have been valid since the beginning of time and will remain valid through eternity. As long as there are beings with the logical structure of mind that humans possess, the laws of human action can effectively guide the actions of men and women. The logical structure of the brain is the most advanced structure we've found in life yet. Your Dynamic Weapons depend on you understanding the laws of human action.

To be not selfish at all would mean certain death in the olden times. But being irrationally greedy would be just as bad. Your peers would have shunned and ignored you, perhaps kicking you out of the tribe. You must distinguish the difference between letting people walk over you and you demanding the World when you're owed Rhode Island.

It's particularly important that you avoid people who engage in self-destructive behavior. You need to be aware of the person who has relinquished all self-esteem and self-respect. It's possible that he (she) has fallen so far that he fails to find glory in any of life's experiences. You unleash the joy of your existence when you become aware of life in all its beauty and ugliness. You probably realize the beauty is in the eye of the beholder. We can probably say the same thing about ugliness. Yes, life soars as a marvelous journey you should love and cherish.

Your Dynamic Anti-Irrational Selfishness Weapon continues to conquer one illusion after another.

The worst part about allowing yourself to be around irrationally selfish people is you could start picking up their traits. That's a personal transformation you don't need. Adopting the ways of someone who is a perpetual failure because of their maladaptive behavioral strategies is certainly no sign of success nor would it appear as a path to providence. Talk about being disarmed.

People who are negative and irrationally selfish bring you nothing but pain and sorrow. Having to listen to constant narcissism and deal with their emotional abuse and put downs slaps your self-worth around. I'm sure you've heard accounts of how the abused person descends into an abuser. Abusive situations can be handed down from generation to generation. When it comes to irrationally selfish and emotionally draining people you just need to stay away from them. There is nothing for you to gain. These parasites will cling onto you, keep you down, and suck you dry. If you hang around too long, the real kick in the teeth or groin comes when the irrationally selfish person leaves you, but not before making sure you've become a weaponless, sad hollow shell of the proud man/woman you were.

The key tenant of the self-destructive individual remains his penchant for constantly sacrificing long term benefits and payoffs for various forms of immediate gratification. Instead of saving money he extravagantly uses credit. He (she) overeats, thinking exercise resides in the dark ages. How about the individual who goes beyond a healthy intake of alcohol and drinks himself into a stupor. These unfortunate souls, the irrationally selfish care only for immediate consumption items that bring them instant feelings of joy and goodness—if that's what you can call it.

We demonstrated that drugs should be legal. It's time to end the drug war. That doesn't mean people should abuse them. Tragically, a person with an extremely short-term mentality considers the continuous use of certain drugs as the gateway to the ultimate self-gratifying scenario. Now that's what we can call an illusion—and we're here to conquer life's illusions.

The Negative Emotions

The self-destructive individual constantly gives in to their inner anger, allowing it to destroy any situation he's in. A weapon in the hands of an angry person becomes quite dangerous. It's important for you to understand that he's oblivious to the fact that the source of his destructive tendencies resides within his own mind. A person who lives in world of illusion believes his problems live on the outside instead of the inside. You don't want to be around this individual when he or she doesn't receive desired good or service. Allowing yourself to become the object of someone's nasty outbursts is dangerous to your mental, emotional and physical well-being. Irrationally selfish people who use anger as coping mechanism allow hatred to fester and grow within. They expect future events to be negative because they skew their expectations through a lens of personal bias.

Whatever you do, don't suffer under the illusion you can change the irrationally selfish person. You can't! Conquering life's illusions requires that you acknowledge reality or it will automatically work against you.

I almost hate to tell you this, but it doesn't stop there. Jealousy is the next stop on the crazy train. I refer to it as the "Green Monster of Relationship Destruction." The jealous person see what others have as something that should be rightfully theirs—for whatever invalid reason. Instead of working and putting in the time, developing themselves, their relationships and their network, the jealous man or woman spends time wallowing in self pity or worse, trying to drag others down to their level so he or she won't have to suffer in misery alone. Time to get your Dynamic Weapon ready.

It's an illusion believing you can somehow handle an irrationally jealous person. You know we are here to conquer life's illusions. If you find yourself in this unhappy situation you need to evacuate the premises immediately. If that's not possible, you must leave as soon as possible.

Let's discover what you risk if you continue a relationship with an insanely jealous person. We need to make sure you never fall for the illusion that things will somehow work out.

You made the fatal mistake of staying in a personal relationship with an insanely jealous person much too long. He (she) displays jealousy towards just about everyone you associate with. Talking to members of the opposite sex (same sex if you're gay) unhappily brings you an emotional response of someone scorned. He feels that he's entitled to everything you own and that includes your money. He attempts to wither your spirit, your basic essence. It suddenly occurs to you that you're involved with a full blown neurotic, an irrationally selfish beast and that he's disarmed you. As they say your goose is cooked. Your only option is to cut your loses immediately. No use sacrificing your mental and emotional well-being along with everything else you lost.

The jealous person forces you down a dark road that only leads to a dead end. Your so-called faithful companion as you move towards emotional oblivion is an insanely jealous person who sucks away your vital energy in states of paranoia. What a horrible way to travel. When the jealous person renders you defenseless, you find yourself in a precarious situation.

What about envious people? When people make envy their basic behavioral foundation, the structure rots from their internal feelings of hatred. Hatred often manifests into needless violence, which can be quite destructive in personal relationships. When it spreads on an international scale, we suffer from a horrible, murderous activity we know as war.

It's good to see something that someone else is using, like a tool or device, then thinking to yourself, "Cool, I really want that!" I don't think that qualifies as envy whatsoever. However, if you suddenly notice extreme negative feelings about that person surfacing, envy is about to expose it's ugly force.

Envy usually grows from the ideals of wealth, health and the family. It's easy to fall into the trap of envy in our tricky world of today. After all, aren't you supposed to keep up with the Jones? Well, it's an illusion thinking you should compare your situation with other people's situation. It's safe to believe that if they did possess any Dynamic Weapons, they sold them for worthless trinkets.

We see wealth spread out more extensively than it was during the Gilded Age/Golden age of colonialism worldwide. We live in the most advanced civilization to ever grace the earth. We've seen technological progress increase to unimaginable levels. Yet we run into people who refuse to learn how to use computers. Intransigent people shun math and English and display irrational resistance to capturing the technical skills that could easily give them exactly what they want. Here are unfortunate people who form the root of the envious.

Do you realize the entitlement mentality that pervades our society reinforces the twisted thoughts and feelings of the envious. These irrationally selfish people feel entitled to whatever they desire. Give him a gift and he won't think of it as a gift. He will view it as something he deserves—and he will demand more from where that came from. If you don't cave in and keep giving him unearned "gifts" he will try to appeal to your feelings of guilt. **Warning:** He has you within his sights, hoping to get the chance to use the deadly irrational selfishness weapon against you. To make matters worse, it's also the Social Altruist's weapon of choice.

You better be alert. Here comes the deadly irrational selfishness weapon—guilt, seeking another victim. It's time to access your Dynamic Anti-Irrational Selfishness Weapon and render his evil weapon permanently impotent. Prepare to Ready, Aim, Fire and repeat.

You conquer another one of life's illusions when you realize that it's impossible to trade value for value with a person who shoots from his envious hip. He takes value without giving any in return.

The Abuser

Abusers use guilt to manipulate people. Those that fall into the guilt trap are liable to believe anything the abuser tells them.

A normal, healthy relationship would never involve one party beating the other party over the head with the weapon of guilt. Your life does not take place in TV courtroom. It takes place in world we call reality. I know. Some metaphysicians claim that life is an illusion. Well, go bang your head against the wall several times and let me know how the illusion feels. We're committed to conquering life's illusions, not proving that life's an illusion.

In order to help you conquer life's illusions we must cover some controversial territory involving religion. I believe spiritual feelings are unique to the individual. Your relationship to God, Allah, Jesus, Buddha, Krishna, Muhammad, Universal Mind, Goddess etc. expresses your connection to all there is. The problem arises when people begin using guilt to force you to believe what they believe. History speaks volumes about the bloodshed religious wars caused.

Crusaders of organized religion have been using guilt since the beginning of time to force people to believe their way. How about the crucifixion of Jesus. Now it's up to you whether or not you believe Jesus soars as the Savior. I'm sure that if you call yourself a Christian the first four books of the New Testament not only inspire you, but provide you spiritual enlightenment. The rest of the New Testament continued your marvelous journey. By the way I read the Bible from start to finish and benefited immensely from the wisdom it supplied me. I'm not attempting to change your religious beliefs, but I am dedicated to helping you use your Dynamic Anti-Irrational Selfishness Weapon to eliminate guilt from your life.

Unfortunately during the Dark Ages, Catholic Priests interpreted the Bible in ways that instilled an incredible amount of fear and guilt into people. I don't think we can call that spiritual. In fact, you were supposed to feel guilty because some unsavory people crucified Jesus. Heck, his disciples couldn't even save him. Poor Peter heard the rooster crow three times, events Jesus told him would happen. *"And Peter remembered the words of Jesus, who said unto him, Before the cock crows, you shall deny me three times. And he went out, and wept bitterly."* Matthew 26:75. Talk about feeling guilt.

We must ask the following question. How does that apply to everyone born after that unhappy event? I know the death and resurrection of Jesus could very well apply to your deep spiritual feelings. However, there exists absolutely no reason you should feel guilt about something other people did. You didn't have anything to do with it.

Then there's the heaven and hell legend. Yes, you certainly can create your heaven or your hell here on earth. In addition we have the tragic spectacle of Social Altruists, do-gooders and world-improvers attempting to turn our great planet into a hell hole.

I hope you don't believe that you're destined for eternity in Hell just because you don't do or believe what religious manipulators tell you to do or believe. These people seek power, wanting to control your body, mind and spirit. Let's face it. Hell is a terribly exploited idea drummed up by the religious in command. People didn't know that much back in the Dark Ages. If a trusted figure told them they would burn in eternal hell fire, these helpless, traumatized, scared souls fervently believed it, as if the priests and judges had an actual fire pit they were throwing people in to.

Isn't obvious to you that evil, power mongering religious fanatics resorted to the widespread manipulation of terror. If guilt plagues your very existence, you must confront it and rid it from your life—and you possess the Dynamic Weapon to do just that. Your life is too important to spend time sabotaging your peace of mind. Let's continue to explore how terrible guilt actually is.

You don't want people and circumstances forcing you into a condition of low self-esteem and sinking self-worth. Once emotional and mental depression captures you, you're on your way to a treatment that includes anti-depressives to restore your natural chemistry. Now that's complete disarmament.

When your life spins out of control, keeping up with normal appearances becomes a challenge. A person suffering from mental and emotional illness runs the risk of joblessness and long-term unemployment. It's hard to accomplish anything worthwhile if you're too depressed to get out of bed. How about personal relationships, enjoying your favorite activities or even appreciating the simple things in life. A depressed individual allows the many pleasures of life to pass right on by. What a tragedy it is when a person lets life push him (her) into depression, grabbing control of life away from his grasp, leaving him a hopeless wreck.

Don't you think it might be rather demoralizing to hang around an extremely depressed person. You don't want his low energy rubbing off on you. What can you do, especially if the person is your sibling, parent, aunt or uncle, in-law, childhood friend or coworker. You will be tempted over and over again to be their keeper, to help them. Now obviously if the depressed individual is your spouse or a family member who lives in your household you are going to have to deal with it. You may need to seek professional help or spiritual counseling.

How about someone outside of your household. Here's where some dangers wait to ambush you. Get your Dynamic Weapon ready for immediate action.

Self-protection becomes vital when you're dealing with someone who falls helplessly into a bottomless pit of depression. If you hold out your hand you risk the danger of the depressed individual pulling you down with them. Here's a scenario for you to carefully consider.

Let's say the person afflicted with depression asks for your help in the form of money or even worse asks if he can stay at your home for free. As far as money is concerned, do not give him (her) any unless you enjoy playing the fool. If you value the person you might help pay some of his bills directly. Whatever you do, don't give him the money to pay the bills. Also make sure you firmly state this is a one time occurrence. **Warning!** Do not offer financial help if it means sabotaging your own financial health. And if the person shows up again you tell him **NO!** And don't feel guilty for taking a firm stand.

How about allowing him to stay in your home. I don't recommend it. However, if you must, set a time limit for him or her in writing, also indicating the person is only a temporary guest. You must realize that some people are almost impossible to get rid of. You don't want to live with an invader. Talk about losing control of your circumstances and your Dynamic Weapons of self defense.

How about helping people who help themselves. Any one of us can find ourselves in a sticky situation. Yes! Helping people who help themselves could supply you with enormous rewards. In addition, you might someday need help. Nothing like building value for value relationships and acquiring valuable allies.

Congratulations, your Dynamic Anti-Irrational Selfishness Weapon just completely conquered the deadly irrational selfishness weapon—guilt. That took incredible courage to render it completely impotent. By the way, consider anything that irrationally selfish people and Social Altruists use against you as something you must conquer. I hesitate to call whatever these misery-mongers attack you with as "weapons" since your Dynamic Weapons will effectively wipe them out.

The World Owes Me a Living

Let's consider the thought process of the delusional person who believes the world owes him a living. Some people can't accept the fact there's no such thing as a free lunch. If you help someone who's plagued with the entitlement mentality, you will see them again and again arriving at your doorstep with both hands out, expecting you to supply their needs. Not a pleasant situation for you to endure time after time.

Don't get me wrong. I believe in helping my friends within the scope of our friendships, but you cannot allow the help to be recurring or extended. People need to figure things out on their own, and the more you meddle in their life the longer it will take them to learn the success lessons of life.

Much of their problems stem from the fact they simply never learned to be successful. Now that's a formula for becoming perpetually depressed. Sadly, it gets to a point where the hapless individual believes that happiness never was meant for him. A lot of times you will help someone and as soon as he (she) begins to see success he sabotages the progress and (or) friendship. You may ask why someone would do that. It's because the neurotic individual doesn't believe he deserves to be happy. Unfortunately, most of the bad programming resides in the subconscious. There's no telling what happened to a person when he was in his formative childhood years. The damaged child lives on, acting from the influence of coping mechanisms and inner monologues. Bad parents leave a child defenseless by disarming him of the weapons he needs to confront the challenges of life.

Experience reigns as the best teacher. When you've dealt with situations like this over and over, they become more and more predictable each time. You don't want a helping situation to emotionally, mentally and spiritually exhaust you. How often does the "help" worsen the situation? You know Social Altruism always causes more problems than it cures. On a personal basis, friendships are frequently destroyed as soon as money enters the picture. If you learn the virtue of saying no (some extremely potent ammo) when appropriate, you will actually strengthen your friendship. If you lose a "friend" by saying no, you discover your so-called friend only considered you a milk cow. However, a friend who understands the virtue of trading value for value soars as someone you can happily help out of a bad situation. If you find yourself experiencing an undesirable circumstance, you know you have a friend who will supply some much needed help. Gratitude and appreciation reside on a road paved with love, compassion and understanding. It's nice feeling that life's not always a series of exhausting battles in a continuous war.

It's demoralizing to discover you're in an arrangement where appreciation vacated the premises. You stupidly stomp on your self-worth and self-esteem when you render your time and money to someone who doesn't appreciate it. Dealing with an irrationally selfish person places you in a hopeless situation. He has less consideration for you than he has for a charitable organization. How do you feel about an unappreciative spouse, child or parent? Why take abuse from someone outside of your household. In fact, why take it from a member of your immediate family. You must discover freedom from irrationally selfish people—or you will sadly discover that you stand naked and weaponless in a world of illusion.

As I stated earlier in the book, Social Altruists are in constant need of irrationally selfish people to help them accomplish their goals—which usually end in social destruction rather than social justice. Who unwittingly looks for Social Altruists to solve their problems? Who is first in line to feast on the banquet of government benefits and handouts? I hope you are becoming efficient at using your Dynamic Weapons. Ready, Aim, Fire.

Irrationally selfish people dive head first into a variety of self-destructive behaviors. Yeah, let's try something that's detrimental to my long-term well being. You never know; this time it might work to my benefit. That's an illusion you need to eradicate from your life—permanently.

Parasites, Government Interventionism and The Fed

How about government handouts? You must face the fact that most social programs exist to satisfy the unearned needs of irrationally selfish people who tend to be sleazy, bossy, greedy individuals.

Because of government interventionism and Federal Reserve easy money schemes, irrationally selfish individuals often end up in chief executive or company president positions. And you wondered why working for Corporate America seems to suck big time. These parasites will grab short-term non-productive returns for their shareholders, often at any and all costs. Once markets collapse because of Fed created boom and bust cycles, they call for bailouts and more easy money, all at your expense. You do realize that economic violating monetary policies such as Quantitative Easing (QE) and Zero Interest Rate Policy (ZIRP) are meant to transfer wealth from Main Street to Wall Street.

Since the self destructive lack self-control and self-sufficiency, they call on Social Altruists to create a government nanny state to take care of them. Imagine selling out your personal liberty and economic freedom for an illusion. You become completely defenseless when you give those up. Believing the government can supply you security rates as a first class illusion, one you must conquer with all of your Dynamic Weapons. How can you possess self-esteem if you accept the illusion that someone else must always be liable, and nobody should be responsible for their actions. Let's not continue to cheer on these economic saboteurs. Can you imagine the power the parasite gains when he receives the sanction of the victim. Ayn Rand states *"The "sanction of the victim" is the willingness of the good to suffer at the hands of the evil, to accept the role of sacrificial victim for the "sin" of creating values."* Your Dynamic Anti-Social Altruism Weapon protects you from this "unhealthy" role. Ready, Aim, Fire

Personal Irrational Selfishness

Here is a question that you must answer to the best of your ability. Can you afford to carry the baggage that irrational selfishness brings? Who needs excess baggage during the chaos of an economic disaster. You must always answer the question with a large, loud and resounding **No!** You can't afford to indulge in irrational selfishness when the streets are covered with "blood." Imagine running around like a chicken with its head cut off, freaking out, not knowing what to do. My god, you would be inviting complete disaster. You lose when you indulge in irrational selfishness and you continue to suffer loses when you hang around irrationally selfish people. Misery loves company and when it comes down to who will survive, the irrationally selfish person will disarm you before throwing you to the wolves. You've heard of the dangers of swimming with the sharks. You don't want to look like one of the idiots who swam in the treacherous waters of Wall Street miscreants.

During harsh times, drug and alcohol use increases. Maybe you can escape your misery for a short while, but you cannot escape reality indefinitely. Moderate indulgence in your pleasures can bring you rewarding satisfaction. Drinking or drugging yourself into oblivion won't cut the mustard. Eventually, reality sends the piper around demanding immediate payment plus compound interest. Harsh demands plus hopelessness sends some people into a suicidal state of mind.

Conquering life's illusions requires that you remain focused. You increase your odds of success when you confront your challenges with a clear mind. Becoming soused or drugged out hampers your ability to make correct decisions and take prompt action. It's rather difficult to Ready, Aim, Fire successfully, when you're mentally and emotionally incapacitated. When you're seriously impaired, your enemies easily disarm you.

I have some important advice for you. Instead of indulging in mind-numbing activities invest in your body, mind and spirit. You certainly don't want to drain the vital energy of your health and mind. I don't have any problem with you smoking a joint or enjoying a few drinks. Remember that overindulgence in any activity takes you to the point of diminishing returns. You don't want to find yourself in the position of having "shot your wad." You're trying to increase your enjoyment of life, not diminish it.

Lifestyle Choices

Another dangerous situation that rears it's ugly head is home entertainment in the form of Cable, Network TV, Amazon Prime, Hulu, Netflix and whatever else you use to watch movies and TV shows. Most of these websites allow you to watch season after season of shows; just one episode after another. Think of how much time you use up every day watching them. Now there's nothing wrong with enjoying your favorites shows or movies. In fact, cuddling up with a loved one or just relaxing while watching something entertaining rewards you with pleasure.

Let's discover the problem with a lifestyle that has you obsessively watching home entertainment.

You should consider your time valuable. Instead of allowing your dreams and ambitions to wither away you could use your precious time to learn a new skill online, write a book (that's what I'm doing) or discover more effective ways to improve your life. You begin conquering life's illusions by increasing the potency of your Dynamic Weapons.

Unfortunately, members of the political establishment merely wish to make citizens comfortable in poverty rather than eliminating poverty. Guess what? If you become completely self-sufficient by conquering life's illusions, you can tell politicians and Social Altruists to go jump in a lake. These purveyors of human misery probably have nightmares about the possibility you will realize you don't need them.

Honestly, how much do you really gain from watching Hell's Kitchen or all of the Kardashian drama? Now I'm not say there's anything wrong with these shows. However, look within and ask the following question. Do the above shows make me a better person? There are hundreds of amazing free courses on websites like Coursera, Udemy, Udacity, and lots of courses even on YouTube. You could spend just a few hours every day on those sites and within six to nine months I guarantee you will improve your skills and your market price. Yes, you will be worth more to potential employers and other people who can help you.

Too many people use drugs and alcohol to numb their immense pain. Sometimes it seems easier to get high than face reality. I understand. I've indulged in irrational selfishness to ease my pain. Fortunately, that's now past me because I've learned to conquer life's illusions. You know what's really fun and rewarding. I'm stilling learning how to conquer illusions. Life's an eternal learning situation.

Until you can face your inner dragons, they will continue to breathe fire at your body, mind and spirit. Even after it appears you've conquered them, another dragon rears it fire snorting head. Life consists of obstacles and challenges. You must be prepared. The only men and women without problems reside in graveyards. Still, if the metaphysicians are right about the afterlife, the challenges and obstacles never go away. Don't you agree that a challenge free life might become quite uninspiring and boring.

Conclusion

Just imagine for a moment living a life of joy and ecstasy. It's your perfect right to enjoy the pleasures of life. The irrationally selfish person has neither joy nor ecstasy in his life and he greatly diminishes his enjoyment of the wonders life has to offer. He feels no gratitude for the gifts of life. In addition, he attempts get by day after day without trading value for value. You can't expect much from other people if you don't have values to offer them. There will be no overcoming hardship for this person. The Rationally Selfish Individual, the impeccable warrior eventually becomes a Master of Life.

Dynamic Weapon #2 just destroyed the irrational selfishness illusion. Let's discover your most potent weapon for conquering life's illusions.

The Rationally Selfish Individual TAKES CHARGE of his thoughts, feelings and actions. He knows all effects have causes, and he makes sure he understands cause and effect relationships. He may error in his judgment, as all men do from time to time, but he has acquired the ability to adjust his thinking and actions. He takes purposive action to achieve his goals and desires.

CHAPTER THREE

DYNAMIC RATIONAL SELFISHNESS WEAPON

In Chapter One, I mentioned that you must avoid the anti-life philosophy of Social Altruism. We learned how Social Altruists completely screw up the very situations they're trying to fix. These purveyors of human misery create a government infrastructure that looks for new problems to mend and new injustices to correct. It's amazing in a sad way how do-gooders and world-improvers never cease to innovate ways to interfere in your life. With people like this around, you must protect your personal liberty and economic freedom with some powerful self-defense techniques. Adolf Hitler's public health campaigns helped cement his power in Nazi Germany. Yes, he was a Social Altruist par excellence.

In Chapter Two, I explained how irrational selfishness in others and yourself could obliterate your success and happiness. Irrationally selfish individuals have terrible interpersonal habits and self-destructive thoughts and behaviors. They're so far behind in the race of life they think they're ahead. How far gone can you get! Fortunately, you're ahead in the race because you now possess two Dynamic Weapons—and your most effective one is on the way.

Conquering life's illusions means shielding your very being from the negative thoughts and words that the irrationally selfish person directs your way. He (she) will also drag you down with other forms of verbal abuse and rights violations. We went over their destructive behavioral and personality traits. In addition we covered the pros and cons of providing help to someone in need. We helped you conquer some of life's illusions by advising you how to handle people who ask for your assistance. I hope you learned how to prevent irrationally selfish people from exploiting you. Obviously, people need to learn how to help themselves.

Let's face it. Irrational selfishness in others and yourself could obliterate your success and happiness. During good times, it causes much mischief and marks the beginning of social and personal decline. During ongoing economic problems, it will prove deadly to your well-being.

The "successful" politician learns that he can pander to and appease irrationally selfish people. Here's where control comes in. When you engineer people to be irrationally selfish you can control them indefinitely. Social Altruists and politicians thrive on the type of person who allows his self-esteem and self-worth to slip to the bottom of an abyss. Nothing like controlling men and women who hopelessly sink to a state of worthlessness. You just met some completely defenseless people who mistaken illusions for reality.

You won't conquer life's illusions if you nosedive to the level of an irrationally selfish person. When the proverbial you know what hits the fan during an economic crisis, you certainly don't want to fall to the level of someone who abandoned his individuality, his self-worth. Sinking to their level guarantees you finally reach the state of equality Social Altruists and Utopians dream about. Yeah, you'll be as equally miserable and poverty stricken as the rest of the reality evaders—and weaponless. Can you imagine how you will feel when the negative emotions of hate, anger, envy and jealousy take over your life. You might even start believing in the illusion of social equality. I guess it could be worse. At least Social Altruists will "love" you. They might even allow you to play in your sandbox with toy guns.

The Tyranny of Irrational Selfishness

As mentioned some irrationally selfish people team up with Social Altruists and join the establishment. We know them as the elite, people who profit from government interventionism and the Fed's egregious monetary policies. Here are the masters of economic mayhem; financial parasites who engineer programs that transfer wealth from Main Street to Wall Street. I know it's tempting to get in on the "game" by joining them. However, you don't want to sell your soul to the devil. The marketplace still offers you plenty of honest ways to profit.

Anyway, you would only hold the illusion that you were permitted into the inner circle of financial games. You would enter a dangerous place where none of your Dynamic Weapons are allowed. When "dinner time" was about to arrive you would wonder why someone placed an apple in your mouth. You would also begin to feel mighty hot. You would think "Man I'm starting to roast." Damn, you realize too late you're the main course. Remember the old Twilight Zone episode "To Serve Man." The episode describes an alien race of Social Altruists who come to earth to serve man. That gets me to thinking. Maybe they're already here. I think I hear the dinner bell ringing.

The majority of irrationally selfish individuals will experience difficulty adapting to market conditions. Most of them lack the ambition or self-discipline to go back to school to learn new skills or even a new profession. It takes time and persistent effort to acquire mathematical, engineering, writing and computer skills. During ongoing economic problems, these people will not only prove to be deadly to their own well-being, but they could very well threaten your life, liberty and property. You might ask how is that possible?

When it gets down to base survival, irrationally selfish people start making incredible demands. Can you believe they actually claim it's the government's responsibility to house and feed them. Here's a Social Altruists dream come true, a dream that envisions a global socialist revolution.

The Bottom Line

You must understand the bottom line. People like this will refuse to take the road out of hell because they'd rather stay in their illusory comfort zone. Your reasoning mind tells you that you must exhibit extreme caution. Misery loves company. The irrationally selfish person will consciously or unconsciously attempt to drag you down to their level of unhappiness and hopelessness. Somewhere deep within a dark place of his (her) psyche, he believes you don't deserve to experience a happy and fulfilling life. You don't want to be cornered when anger, hate, fear, envy and jealousy rear their ugly heads. Imagine finding yourself in the unenviable position of hopelessly trying to cut off the heads of the Hydra of Lema. You're better off cutting your loses and vacating the premises. Once you're adept at using your Dynamic Weapons to conquer life's illusions you will avoid these types of situations.

I admit that modern life places us in some tricky situations. After all, these are particularly treacherous times in which we live. So what exactly are you supposed to do about it? It's possible you wonder what will become of our once great nation. Maybe, you fear for the safety of you and your loved ones. I can certainly understand if you feel some uneasiness about possible interactions with irrationally selfish people, especially after we exposed how dangerous they can be to your well-being. You'll be happy to know that a solution awaits you. You're in for a real treat. Soon, we will conquer a gigantic illusion by supplying you with an almost unbelievable Dynamic Weapon.

In order to survive and thrive during good times and bad times you have to keep your eye on the ball or we could say the reality of each situation. If at all possible do not deal with a person who acts in an irrationally selfish manner. Especially don't allow him or her into your personal life. You certainly don't want an energy vampire to suck you dry. There's also a good chance he will drain your financial health. Your Dynamic Weapons aren't too effective once your ammo disappears. You don't need any of that misery.

Once you eliminate irrationally selfish people from your life, you'll notice a cleansing of your body, mind and spirit. However, you might first suffer some withdrawals. You probably didn't realize you became attached to someone who was bad for you. Happily you will wake up one morning and noticed that you are free to be you, the most important person in the world.

You have the natural right to the pursuit of life, liberty and happiness. You deserve to experience personal liberty and economic freedom. Understand that irrationally selfish people aren't just manipulative and annoying but they violate your basic human rights. Conquering life's illusions means you make every effort to eliminate these people from your life.

Okay, you're probably wondering what type of person possesses the strength to overcome challenges caused by personal difficulties and continuous economic crisis.

Are you ready for the shocking and somewhat controversial answer? He exists as the Rationally Selfish Individual. He lives life as the impeccable warrior. In fact you excel as the warrior and the Dynamic Weapon.

Traits of the Rationally Selfish Individual

Conquering life's illusions requires you to accept an eternal truth. Here it is. All people act in what they believe to be their own best interest. There are no exceptions. Everyone acts from selfishness. I hope that wasn't too hard to swallow. Now let's narrow it down.

A large difference exists between irrational selfishness and Rational Selfishness. In fact the gulf is quite wide. Whether you like it or not that's the way it is. I know. It's difficult for people to accept that selfishness rules human nature. Even kind-hearted gentle people act from self-interest. The Saint wouldn't attempt to act for the good of all if it wasn't in his best interest. By the way don't confuse Saints and highly spiritual individuals with Social Altruists. You just discovered that Rational Selfishness actually benefits people. The irrational selfishness of Social Altruists benefits the few at the expense of everyone else. Isn't conquering life's illusions fun.

The Rationally Selfish Individual shuns and exposes the anti-life philosophy of Social Altruism because he knows of the catastrophic consequences it has caused and will continue to cause. Here's your first opportunity to brandish your Dynamic Rational Selfishness Weapon. Ready, Aim, Fire.

He (she) would never purposely behave in an irrationally selfish manner. He TAKES CHARGE of his thoughts, feelings and actions. He knows all effects have causes, and he makes sure he understands cause and effect relationships. He may error in his judgment, as all men do from time to time, but he has acquired the ability to adjust his thinking and actions. He takes purposive action to achieve his goals and desires.

The Warrior and the Dynamic Rational Selfishness Weapon

An individual who practices Rational Selfishness realizes he possesses power. He (she) is an individualist, an impeccable warrior. He takes complete responsibility for his thoughts, feelings and actions, and confidently accomplishes his goals and desires. He eliminates negative feelings of anger, hate, envy and jealousy from his being. He confidently accomplishes his goals and desires.

His actions harmonize with his values. He definitely wouldn't consider accepting the second-hand values of others. He has complete confidence in the efficacy of his mind and he takes purposive action. Can you imagine an individual of this caliber lamenting the sad fact he doesn't know where his thoughts and feelings come from or why he acts on them in self-destructive ways.

Here's what's nice. Once you adopt the role of the Rationally Selfish Individual you capture control of your mind. You excel at reconciling your life to your surroundings. Plain and simple, your effectiveness in dealing with life's challenges and obstacles increase. It becomes virtually impossible for you to stumble towards mental instability or act out of line with your ethical beliefs. The warrior and the weapon become one. The Rationally Selfish Individual manifests as a Dynamic Weapon. Yes! You soar as the Dynamic Rational Selfishness Weapon.

Let's conquer another one of life's illusions. Events in your life don't just happen willy-nilly. You must understand that your conscious and subconscious thoughts determine your outcome. In other words, your mind creates your life before the results manifest in reality. Right now you are creating your future and you may be creating it unconsciously. The Rationally Selfish Individual increases his awareness and begins consciously creating his life.

The Warrior's Code

The Impeccable Warrior TAKES CHARGE of his thoughts, feelings and actions. He happily discovers cause and effect relationships in the sphere of human action. His sense of life allows him to experience the joy of his existence.

Self-Mastery means the individual knows he exists as a being who possesses power. It is possible to call him or her a warrior. In the classic book by Carlos Castaneda, "Journey to Ixtlan" don Juan says "A warrior calculates everything. That's control. But once his calculations are over he acts. A warrior is not a leaf at the mercy of the wind. No one can push him; no one can make him do things against himself or against his better judgment. A warrior is tuned to survive, and he survives in the best of all possible fashions."

Not only does the impeccable warrior tune himself to survive, he (she) thrives. He understands reality and he uses his knowledge to succeed in his endeavors. The warrior obtains peace of mind because he is confident in his ability to overcome challenges and obstacles. He believes that he will achieve his goals and desires. You can see why Social Altruists and irrationally selfish people fear the existence of the Rationally Selfish Individual. He (she) exists as the most powerful Dynamic Weapon on earth.

Life continually presents you choices. Your success rides on your ability to make more correct decisions than incorrect ones. That's especially true when you're faced with big decisions. You know, the ones that can make or break you. If you decide to live the life of the Rationally Selfish Individual and enjoy the existence of the warrior, I'm ready to supply you some potent ammo.

1. Continue to seek new thoughts and new ideas. So many people shut themselves out when all they need to do is open up and look out. Study the great masters of economics, philosophy and metaphysics, and even look up contrary arguments to those teachings. You should always be on the outlook for more information, never taking anything for granted, and never fully believing everything you hear. You're free to question anything I tell you. You must continue to exercise your mind, expanding it into unknown territory

    You might want to learn a new language or how to play a musical interest. If you have a culinary interest you could learn how to cook or discover new methods of food preparation. Life offers you an unlimited amount of interests for learning and pleasure. Constantly expose yourself to new materials and make your life a continuous quest for success and fulfillment. The government might attempt to reward ignorance; however conquering life's illusions requires you to realize the modern world penalizes it—severely. It's your life and it deserves the best you can give it.

You live in a quickly changing and fast paced world. Something taken for granted such as an idea becomes outdated or even contradicted. A new product or service renders other products and services obsolete. However, remember that wisdom remains eternal. Quite often new ideas defy reality. The Rationally Selfish Individual can distinguish the different between reliable old fashioned wisdom and new-fangled nonsense. You have to allow yourself to grow with the world. It's rather difficult to swim upstream. Still, you don't want to float down a river of ignorance with irrationally selfish people. Ignorance or unfocused desires compromise the survival of the individual during tough times by disarming him. The day arrives when the merciless piper demands payment plus compound interest from those who evade reality.

2. Eat and Exercise for optimum health. If you don't take proper care of your body, eventually not much else will matter. Nobody including you is invincible. I know that it's difficult to think about your morality. However, if you don't start doing all the little things to live better and healthier, an early date with the grave may be likely. It is irrationally selfish not to keep yourself in good mental and physical shape. How you treat yourself could indicate how you will treat others. Do your best to maintain your weight and appearance. You're better off avoiding junk food. Instead eat balanced meals. I also recommend exercising 3 days a week. A brisk walk 4 to 5 days a week will help you stay in shape. Some believe your body is the "Temple of God." You certainly don't want to treat your temple with the disrespect of neglect and abuse. The wise man believes in cleaning his Dynamic Weapons.

The Rationally Selfish Individual understands that his overall health and well-being can affect his environment which includes his employment, productivity, capabilities, awareness and even his relationships. He knows that when you feel good your

durability and energy level soars. A person of this caliber has a better chance of holding a job, increasing productivity and working longer hours when needed. That's what you call adaptability. He (she) sets in motion permanent long-term success.
3. Make meditation or inner reflection a daily experience. I advise meditating in the morning for at least 30 minutes. Personally I prefer an hour of meditation. At the end of the day it is wise for you to reflect on what you accomplished or didn't accomplish. Did any pleasant surprises help you along the way? Did anything unexpected throw a monkey wrench into your plans? If you simply begin doing a daily tracking of the above, you will be that much closer to existing as a Rationally Selfish Individual, an impeccable warrior.

Once you learn to TAKE CHARGE of your thoughts, feelings and actions you take control of your life and your destiny. During tough times this becomes extremely critical. When the tides are low, one wrong move could have you beached. Now that's appears to be a rather helpless situation. The Rationally Selfish Individual acts in a cool, calm manner when faced with adversity—even when the adverse circumstances seem almost too much to handle. He doesn't join the crowd of people who begin losing their heads, giving into hate, anger, jealousy and envy. An unfocused mob can go mad, plundering and pillaging the community around them. You've seen the results in news stories. When it comes down to it you are able to act as the individualist acts. You TAKE CHARGE of yourself and the situation. Meditation and reflection accelerates your ability to gain the necessary skills to handle difficult circumstances. When you control your thoughts, feelings and actions, you TAKE CHARGE of your environment and your destiny. You exist as the Rationally Selfish Individual and the Dynamic Weapon. Ready, Aim, Fire.

I would like to point out there's no such thing as perfection in the sphere of human action. No man or woman is 100% Rationally Selfish. So be kind to yourself and avoid the perfectionist mentality.

Some people waver between Rational Selfishness and irrational selfishness. You need to understand that it's easier to form bad habits than good habits. If you believe you can act as an impeccable warrior acts half the time and succeed in your endeavors you're badly mistaken. You must practice Rational Selfishness the majority of the time or you will hopelessly stumble back into irrationally selfish behavior. Your goal is to consistently act from Rational Selfishness. If you slip up, pull out your Dynamic Weapons, Ready, Aim, Fire—and get back into the zone.

Conclusion

You are now on your way to experiencing the joy of your existence. Now we move towards conquering another one of life's illusions. It's important that you survive and thrive during hard economic times. In the next chapter, I discuss the only social system that can insure the survival of "The American Way of Life", the social system you must endorse and support wholeheartedly to guarantee your survival. It's the Dynamic Weapon of choice for the man and woman of logic and reason.

The Dynamic Weapon of Rational Selfishness will always be your best friend. Along with your other Dynamic Weapons, you need to use it without hesitation against Social Altruists and irrationally selfish people who attempt to steal your personal liberty and economic freedom.

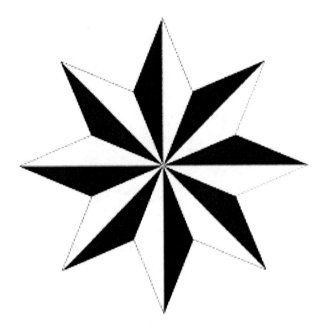

The Rationally Selfish Individual would never support predatory, exclusive, and extractive economic policies. He (she) recognizes that those systems bring short-term benefits by bleeding real wealth from the economy. In the end, an exclusive class (that grows deadly and more compact day by day) enjoys their spoils in an ivory tower built with the blood and bones of the average citizen.

CHAPTER FOUR

DYNAMIC UNHAMPERED CAPITALISM WEAPON

Here is a disturbing truth that I would like to share with you. The Federal Reserve System, Member Banks, The Federal Income Tax, and the Import-Export Bank all exist for one purpose and one purpose only, to transfer wealth from productive citizens to special interests. Of course, Social Altruists and members of the elite claim it's all for the good of society. It makes you wonder where the lovers of personal liberty and economic freedom belong. We can assume us regular citizens were somehow kicked out of the social organization. All productive citizens must be disarmed of their *Dynamic Unhampered Capitalism Weapon without their knowledge. In fact, you're not supposed to know its missing. Even worse, you're not supposed to believe in it.

*Some people refer to this weapon as the Dynamic Laissez Faire Capitalism Weapon or the Dynamic Free Enterprise Weapon. Since Social Altruists hate capitalism and get their kicks hampering your personal liberty and economic freedom we will call it the Dynamic Unhampered Capitalism Weapon.

Before we supply you with the above mentioned Dynamic Weapon, we need to let you know what you're up against. We're dealing with some powerful forces. Evil gains prominence from the sanction of the victims.

The Enemy – The Disastrous Federal Reserve System

Since 1913 the Federal Reserve has done nothing in terms of solidifying the economy. Its manipulation of interest rates spawns destructive boom and bust cycles. Politicians, Social Altruists, government bureaucrats as well as the mainstream media work to destroy the American Capitalistic system so they can form an exclusive economic zone that cements their position at the top. You do realize this is not free enterprise but a complete bastardization of capitalism. Members of the political and financial establishment viciously attack the American Way of Life. These misery mongers foster one economic crisis after another with the intent of creating a divided, entrenched impoverished people who rely on the Government for their very existence. I don't think I have to tell you who stirs up our race relation problems. The race card is part of their plan for dividing people and weakening the social structure.

If you are under the illusion that our institutions exist to serve the people, I hope the above helped you conquer it. That's what we're here for, to conquer life's illusions. And you possess the Dynamic Weapons to slay the enemy.

I think we should look no further than the facts of the matter. The purchasing power of the US Dollar is less than 5% of the purchasing power of the US Dollar in 1913. Gold went from $20.67 per ounce to more than $1100 per ounce, even though members of the financial establishment have done everything in their power to suppress its price. There's no telling how high gold will soar once the manipulations of the elite fail. Even the most powerful people on earth are denied the ability to circumvent Economic Law indefinitely.

Do you wonder who benefits from the continuous depreciation of the dollar. The Fed creates their easy money schemes hoping you chase economic bubbles. The sheeple (combination of words sheep and people) must be sheared. Believing you should chase economic bubbles is one of life's illusions. Let's find out why.

Each Fed created bubble displays similar patterns. By the way, here's where the screwing of the average man (woman) begins. The "In Crowd" receives the newly created money, first investing it in an entire asset & market class. You must understand that these investors gain the support of the Mainstream Media and other sources of manipulation. Eventually media shills convince Main Street USA to invest in a hot market after it is seriously overbought. Guess who pulls out in a classic pump and dump fashion. Members of the elite get rich and you feel like a first class sucker. You must realize that the pattern couldn't take place without the help of the Federal Reserve System. Ron Paul makes sense. It is time to End the Fed.

We can conclude that the Fed attacks your financial well-being. Its most ardent supporters are Social Altruists and irrationally selfish people. Fortunately, you possess the Dynamic Weapons necessary to provide adequate protection against this evil force. Unfortunately, some of their policies remain beyond your control.

One word of advice. In the long-run the Fed's paper promises are worthless. Only hard assets such as gold, silver, land and fine art preserve your wealth. Now that's some effective ammo. If your means are limited, I recommend one ounce American Silver Eagles or Junk Silver (pre 1965) coins.

Conquering Another Enemy – Government Interventionism

What's strange is that it has happened so frequently you'd think we would notice the pattern. Possessing such powers of manipulation allow members of the elite to run a sham democratic system they easily rig through a variety of methods.

Let's conquer another of life's illusions by exposing the Big Lie. Government interventionism benefits the average citizen because it tames the defects of capitalism. **Truth:** Government interventionism benefits members of the political and financial establishment—at your expense.

The American voter thinks he stands a chance of bringing about positive change by choosing between two candidates. Now that's an illusion you have to conquer. I bet you thought you had choice between a Democrat and a Republican. I have some news for you. There's one major party called the Demopublican Party. Members of the political establishment sure pulled a fast on on you. In reality, you didn't really have a choice. The facts and statistics speak for themselves. People unwittingly supported the neutering and massacre of the middle class in America.

You know that what you don't learn through wisdom you learn through woe. In this day and era it seems that wisdom is in short supply, and people stand as martyrs inflicting unnecessary woe upon themselves by refusing to learn lessons from the past. It's wise to notice that history can repeat itself. George Santayana said *"Those who cannot remember the past are condemned to repeat it."* Woe has opened its doors to many people, inviting them to step right in and suffer through harsh economic times and unfortunate situations of economic despair.

As the Bible states: *"but the children of the kingdom shall be cast out into outer darkness: there shall be weeping and gnashing of teeth* (Matthew 8: 11-12)." It pains me to acknowledge that this could be the nightmare of many for years to come. Your Dynamic Weapons should protect you from that undesirable fate.

The Department of Uneducation

In order to conquer illusions we attempt to accurately describe problems the United States and her people will face for years to come. How about our faltering educational system. Standardized testing, the Department of Education and Common Core continue to deliver fatal blows. We suffer through a decline in the quality of education that has no other precedent in modern society. Social Altruists and vested interests lower standards to the mean of the students sitting on the bottom of the scale. You might wonder why they would attempt to guarantee mediocrity and less. Everyone must pass because it looks very bad on schools flunking people and having 5th or 6th grade seniors hanging around. So instead of owning up to the mess, the educational system (if that's what you can call it) incentivizes administrative ways around the problems. As you can see the incentivized administration creates more problems than it solves. It's much easier to solve something if you get to the core of problem immediately. We know that that's beyond the capabilities of an educational bureaucracy. No wonder home schooling seems to be catching on.

Since the implementation of the Department of Education (Uneducation) in 1979, we have failed to see lasting improvements in education. The drop in standards should shock Social Altruists and educational bureaucrats. Unfortunately, these destroyers of the educational system either deny reality or possess ulterior motives. How can they not recognize how much their detrimental educational policies smackdown learning. Colleges graduate students who wouldn't have cut the mustard 15-20 years ago.

Are we being harsh when we claim some of the students who graduated should have flunked out? Possibly. But it isn't any harsher than giving a child the false confidence that he or she has what it takes to succeed in a college or post-college environment. There are many occupations that don't require going into debt for an "education" that might not further the student's best interest. You can imagine the rude awakening some students receive when they are slammed into College. Entering an arena of higher learning must cause incredible stress to someone completely unprepared for the reality of his situation. Social Altruists don't care if they set someone up for failure. These do-gooders feed on the carcasses of the weak.

I put on my sheeple's clothing and purposely ran into a Social Altruist. He thought he had me by the balls. I immediately removed my disguise, showed him my Dynamic Rational Selfishness Weapon and displayed my Dynamic Anti-Social Altruism Weapon. He practically melted away. He kept babbling "You must be kept dumb. You must be kept dumb." What does that tell you? It tells you that he just revealed a core part of his anti-life philosophy.

The Tragedy of Private Prisons

We can observe the tragic results of setting up our kids for failure. In despair some of our young people end up in black market activities, another sorry situation created by our government. Eventually, too many of these unfortunate souls end up in an evil institution we call a private prison. Instead of a receiving proper, life-enhancing education, he ends up as slave labor earning profits for private prison stockholders. Do you wonder what kind of person would invest in other people's misery. It's enough to believe the devil's disciples have taken over our planet. Evidence seems to indicate they've taken over Wall Street and the US government. Damn, that ought to piss you off. Now don't go berserk with your Dynamic Weapons. The Rationally Selfish Individual TAKES CHARGE of his thoughts, feelings and actions. Ready, Aim, Fire.

Inmates are placed into situations where they are exposed to extremely hazardous cancer causing chemicals. The company that exposed them to the carcinogens gets completely off the hook. After all, these violators of human rights believe prisoners possess no basic rights and should be worked to death or to the point where cancer renders then unproductive. Now we're not saying that we're soft on crime, although we believe there should be no laws against voluntary exchanges. In other words, there should be no victimless crime laws. Private prisons exist to earn profits. The more people our injustice system can incarcerate the more money private prisons make. That's what you call a sorry situation. You can imagine how many Dynamic Weapons the Warden allows the inmates. Still, you must realize that nobody can take away your Dynamic Rational Selfishness Weapon. If you find it missing, it means you inadvertently lost it through non-use or you stupidly disarmed yourself.

You can see how we treat the lowest members of society. The educational mishaps of the Department of Education add fuel to the private prisoner fire. The anti-life philosophy of the Social Altruist states that the more marginalized kids you can alienate through educational butchery the better. I guess you can say that the educational system succeeded in creating a cheap source of labor, with up to 80% of inmates in jail for victimless crimes. Conquering your illusions means you realize that you face life in a system the elite rigged in their favor. Fortunately, the Rationally Selfish Individual learns how to successfully deal with adversity. Napoleon Hill said *"Every adversity, every failure, every heartache carries with it the seed of an equal or greater benefit."* His wisdom remains true, unless of course you make a fatal mistake.

Our Conquering Ways Continue

Are you familiar with Keynesian economists. Incredibly these quack economists believe you can spend your way to prosperity. In addition, they display an irrational fear of increased savings and lower prices. What's really scary is that these economic nitwits control the Federal Reserve System. Their inflationary policies in the form of Quantitative Easing (QE) and Zero Interest Rate Policy (ZIRP) slowly but surely convert Americans into slaves. And you thought our government abolished slavery. From the days of the old South up to today, slavery has actually increased. You're probably asking "How can that be true?"

Conquering life's illusions means we hit you with the truth. After the end of the civil war, and especially after the creation of the Federal Reserve System and the Federal Income Tax in 1913, legal slavery ascended from the dustbin of old style slavery. People are under the control of the powers in ways they cannot even comprehend. Sadly, members of the establishment transformed us into financial slaves. The swindle of 0% interest rates makes it extremely difficult for you to save money. In addition, a high percentage of the money you thought you successfully invested gets pilfered in each Federal Reserve created financial crisis.

You can expect boom-bust cycles about every 5 to 7 years, although they can occur more or less frequently. The system encourages you to spend and spend more money even if you have to accumulate humongous amounts of debt to do it. Ka Ching! The Social Altruists in the system view this as necessary for the foundation of a modern or moral society. Talk about a perverted moral system. I fail to see the conversion of the largest free population in history into the largest slave population ever as morally or economically desirable. When a free man suddenly come up against a slave master it's time to Ready, Aim, Fire.

The Plans of Social Altruists and the Irrationally Selfish

"The best laid plans of mice and men go oft astray."
Robert Burns

I've noticed over the years that Social Altruists, politicians and government bureaucrats design poorly laid plans, doomed to failure because they pollute them with fatal flaws. The reason we can call them fatal flaws stems from the fact that the so-called do-gooders root them in deeply held economic illusions. People who live in a world of illusion often confuse their unsubstantiated personal beliefs with reality. Now that fatal illusion deals death blows to your personal liberty and economic freedom. You cannot allow someone's illusions to disarm you.

We are here to conquer personal illusions. Beliefs that fail to ground themselves in reality cannot succeed. In fact, the unhappy results manifest in abject failure.

Let's present you some information you will find difficult to swallow. Some Social Altruists purposely attack your individual rights. Yes, that's right. They foster failure in order to accumulate power at your expense. These creators of human misery toss you bait in the form of social schemes, claiming they're for the "good of society." Once hapless citizens take the bait, they become hopelessly aligned with economic situations that include inflation, crippling government regulations, debilitating wars, confiscation of savings, violations of personal liberty and freedom, etc. etc. When you're hooked, you suffer through a vicious cycle of seeing your values vanish into nothingness. Actually many of your dreams and desires end up in the possession of members of the political and financial establishment. Now you can see the importance of your Dynamic Anti-Social Altruism Weapon.

The Biggest Scam Ever

Are you ready for the shocking truth. According to David Stockman one time budget director for Ronald Reagan and author of "The Great Deformation: The Corruption of Capitalism in America" "Maybe 100,000 people "live large" off today's $95 trillion casino. By contrast, according to the Social Security Administration's wage records, there were 100 million workers who held any kind of paying job during 2013, who earned a collective total of just $1.65 trillion that year." And it's getting worse. The establishment has pulled what rates as the biggest scams in the history of mankind.

When someone wakes up in the morning with unpleasant thoughts of just surviving another day, thriving and living life to its fullest becomes rather difficult. Honestly, most people have little to no chance at succeeding inside of the corrupt system. Plus, the average man and woman allows personal illusions to hamper his or her effectiveness in dealing with life's challenges. Fortunately, you are acquiring the necessary Dynamic Weapons to conquer life's illusions.

The hampered market system manifests as a greater and greater downturn for the middle class. To put it bluntly, the evil bastards rob you blind. Don't ever believe your government exists to help you. If you accept that illusion, you might as well surrender. The only kind of 'help" you will receive from a member of the establishment resembles a situation where a "doctor" purposely breaks both of your arms, sets the bones (crookedly) and then demands gratitude and payment for his services.

Social Altruists offer the masses "incentive" programs such as Welfare and Food Stamps that replace the economic opportunities they eliminate with their quack social and economic programs. When wages plummet and the prospect of rewarding employment shrinks, it makes economic sense for people on the borderline to quit working. When I used the word incentive I exposed the establishment doublespeak. Social incentives actually mean that your incentive to better your life will be destroyed. Our "beloved" government now protects you from real life. I guess ignorance is bliss and illusions are life-enhancing. Well Social Altruists, politicians, government bureaucrats and money changers didn't count on people like you conquering life's illusions.

We've seen the middle class decline since 2000 on an unprecedented scale. The conquistadors didn't die, they just came back to life in another form, wearing suits and ties. Let's allow David Stockman to explain the consequence of Zero Interest Rate Policy (ZIRP) and Quantitative Easing (QE). "Instead, this giant $95 trillion pool is where honest savings from the household and business sectors go to be scalped, appropriated and stolen by the hedge funds, dealers, financial engineers and gamblers which populate the casino. It is the excess girth of it that does the damage, magnifying the rent extraction and dead weight economic costs by orders of magnitude." As you can see the more "funny money" the Fed pushes out the better it is for the elite.

Artificially low interest rates create boom and bust cycles. And guess who gets fleeced in the establishment's deceitful circle game. You must understand that a real higher interest rate prevents malinvestments, bad projects from being funded. It also stops what David Stockman described in the previous paragraph. Wouldn't it be nice if an honest market rate of interest resulted in high quality companies that would satisfy the consumers' most urgent desires on a national and global scale. Instead of Central Bankers (Banksters) creating unstable economies and human misery we would begin seeing a worldwide elimination of poverty. Now we have the spectacle of bankers and investors funding inside-circle people with whatever project they come up with regardless of how stupid it is. It might have occurred to you that stupid doesn't seem too profitable. In world where most everything gets turned upside down the parasites reap unearned benefits. You know how you must handle parasites.

Banksters, I mean bankers push money into the system through high risk loans, ones that have a fair chance of collapsing. Here's where the game of hot-potato begins. Bankers loan out the money to their buddies, taking their fee/percentage. The fiat (phony) money moves through the economy reaching the sordid market places that David Stockman describes. The cronies reap a fortune while the ones who end up with the hot potatoes become know as suckers. The Rationally Selfish Individual avoids playing the role of a lollipop. During the 2007 financial crisis some bankers were given negative interest rates. How sinister can it get? It was a slush fund on international scale. The resulting hangover has continued to drag the American middle class down to the point of no return. It appears people will be crying in their beer, singing the "Bailout Blues."

If we continue to allow Central Bankers (Banksters), politicians and Social Altruists to plunder our wealth, we'll have to bring back a golden oldie sung by the great Ray Charles. Here's the first verse of "Busted."

> "My bills are all due and the baby needs shoes and I'm busted.
> Cotton is down to a quarter a pound, but I'm busted.
> I got a cow that went dry and a hen that won't lay.
> A big stack of bills that gets bigger each day.
> The county's gonna haul my belongings away cause I'm busted."

There you have it. Fortunately you exist as a Rationally Selfish Individual, committed to conquering life's illusions.

Let's face the harsh reality that Social Altruism is not a loving, giving philosophy. It tragically manifests as a cannibalistic philosophy of self-sacrifice. In fact, it destroys the sublime values necessary for the well-being of the human race, which is why it is anti-life. Thank God for the

Dynamic Anti-Social Altruism Weapon.

Unfortunately, delusional people seldom relinquish their delusions. Everything government does to "alleviate" the economic blues will only worsen the situation, taking illogic to its logical conclusion, eventual economic breakdown.

Sadly, we have become a nation of the irrationally selfish. We want it now—regardless of whether we have produced or earned it. Many Americans demand instant gratification, instead of planning and saving for the future. The establishment's favorite economist John Maynard Keynes said "In the long run we are all dead." Even though he is dead, the rest of us are now reaping the effects of his spurious economic theories. Governments "thrive" by ignoring the long-run consequences of their policies. I'm sure you realize that most people live their life as if tomorrow never comes. Irrational selfishness runs amuck. You know what Dynamic Weapon comes in handy when your confronted with irrational selfishness.

Unhampered Capitalism and the Rationally Selfish Individual

Markets rule everything. That is the unvarnished truth. The Rationally Selfish Individual supports the social system of unhampered capitalism due to logic, reason, and empirical data. He owns and uses the Dynamic Unhampered Capitalism Weapon. He builds and models it from a social system based on logic, reason and solid economic policies.

The Rationally Selfish Capitalist exists as a neutral and benevolent person. He desires value for value relationships. He loves to see honest exchanges benefit as many deserving people as possible. He thrills to idea of men and women capturing happiness through personal liberty and economic freedom. Yes! You possess a weapon the protects people from the social schemes of Social Altruists and irrationally selfish people.

The Rationally Selfish Individual would never support predatory, exclusive, and extractive economic policies. He (she) recognizes that those systems bring short-term benefits by bleeding real wealth from the economy. In the end, an exclusive class (that grows deadly and more compact day by day) enjoys their spoils in an ivory tower built with the blood and bones of the average citizen. Imagine owning the privilege of making all the policy decisions while effectively shielding yourself from the real world.

We can't consider members of the elite Rationally Selfish Individuals because they gain wealth at the expense of innocent people. Irrationally selfish people hold hands with Social Altruists in a relationship that allows them to gain unearned benefits. Imagine the gall of believing that you deserve to "manage" other people's money. Sociopaths can justify all kinds of nasty schemes.

In order to avoid confusion, we don't consider fabulously wealth people who gain riches by satisfying consumer desires members of the elite. In fact, these men and women deserve our admiration because they become wealthy by trading value for value.

Members of the elite thrive and become wealthy through application of the establishment's political and financial scams. They don't trade value for value. They extort value.

Social Altruism, Government Interventionism and Injustice

You will not find a Rationally Selfish Individual positioned in exclusive economic zones that seek to drain the lower classes. Value for value relationships are more to his liking. Your Dynamic Unhampered Capitalism Weapon defends productive people regardless of social class.

One of the main problems with Social Altruists and irrationally selfish people lies in the interventionist and socialist governments they create. Their evil purpose in life is to extract productive people's resources, eventually bleeding them dry. In this case, the parasite kills the host. That's why social systems eventually collapse, just as the Western Roman Empire and the Mayan Empire bit the dust. A smaller and smaller exclusive class of parasites suck the life out of a system until there's nothing left, even for them. I guess there's some justice in the end when the perpetrators of human suffering are rendered worthless. How can you be on a high horse when you've destroyed the wealth of the people holding you up?

8 Dynamic Weapons for Conquering Life's Illusions

The Rationally Selfish Individual recognizes real social injustice—and it isn't the type that Social Altruists conjure up. Do-gooders, world-improvers, politicians and government bureaucrats turn everything upside down and inside out. In their world of illusion, justice = injustice and visa versa. Fortunately, you possess the Dynamic Weapons to repel that BS. Ready, Aim, Fire.

As a Rationally Selfish Individual you will clearly see that the altruistic government system unfairly redistributes wealth from those who earn it to those haven't earned it. We go from capital accumulation to capital consumption. Now that's a method to prevent new startup businesses from getting off the ground. The Rationally Selfish Individual knows that government interventionism always ends in failure and in fact causes more problems than it solves. Politicians and Social Altruists deliver deep gashing wounds to the economy, then attempt to cover them up with a cheap band-aid. A perceptive individual can observe the life blood of prosperity and well-being flowing freely out of the wound. The professional politician will call for blood thinners to stop the gushing flow of blood. You are probably thinking "This doesn't make sense" You're right. It doesn't make sense.

The Rationally Selfish Individual learns that government interventionism on the marketplace robs people in the name of Social Altruism. The Fed's currency schemes also achieve the same result.

As a Rationally Selfish Individual you will know government theft when you see it and you definitely won't fall for Federal Reserve money scams. Yeah, you'll know when it's time to Ready, Aim, Fire. Every financial crisis is made worse by the Fed, not better. Bogus stimulus programs pile bad money on top of bad money. Anyway, the Fed's manipulation of interest rates usually creates the crisis. Nothing like calling on an arsonist to put out fires. We can conclude that it's time to End the Fed—permanently.

Government *does* have a legitimate function: or series of functions. It exists to protect an individual's life, liberty, and property. The government protects every member of the population the same as the other, regardless of sex, gender, ethnicity, language, disabilities. All stand equal before the law. Unfortunately, the government fails miserably in its only legitimate function. Social Altruists have mucked up the works.

It's becomes increasingly clear how important your Dynamic Anti-Social Altruism Weapon is.

The Rationally Selfish Individual supports the rights of the minority by standing up for individual rights. Yes, the smallest minority happens to be the lone individual. Of course, taking this stand could result in race baiters marginalizing you and painting you as the bad guy. However, you understand that individual rights means everyone is a member of society. As a Rationally Selfish Individual you wholeheartedly root for the lone individual to successfully move forward, even if he currently resides on the bottom of society's totem pole. Still, you oppose the government "helping" him with other people's money. You understand the struggling individual finds his best chance to advance if the government restricts its activities to protecting his (her) life, liberty and property. And let's not forget the pursuit of happiness. If you are for individual rights you are for minority rights. You soar as a real supporter of human rights. Social Altruists fall down as pretenders to the human rights throne.

Some people think that we can completely dispense with governments. That's a happy thought. There's a large group of legitimate people who not only think that the government is a burden but that it is also 100% unnecessary. One group I sympathize with is known as Anarcho-Capitalists. In theory it sounds interesting as it desires a self policing community and promotes tighter knit populations.

We need to ask the following question. Are we successful because of government or despite government? The movement for the latter has increased exponentially under the Presidency of Barack Obama.

We can base a strong argument for the elimination of government on economic facts and data. Government interventionism continues to destroy your personal liberty and economic freedom. Along with the Federal Reserve debauchery of the dollar, our government seems intent on permanently killing our economic system. The same phenomena takes place worldwide as Central Banks and heavy-handed government policies threaten to take down the international economic system. The American market could go out with a bang or it could go the way of the Roman Empire with a whimper. Either way, your Dynamic Rational

Selfishness Weapon gains vital importance.

Some theorists and Utopians believe that government will finally vanish. Karl Marx believed that socialism would cause the State to wither away. What an illusion. The facts demonstrate that socialism creates a totalitarian government. Maybe the disappearance of government could be the natural way of things.

Star Trek, Star Wars and Economic Systems

I like Star Trek, but the cold future of socialism it shows seems completely unrealistic. Socialism causes societies to regress not expand. How about a future with an open society based on "credits." How about Star Wars?

Star Wars comes to life with economic systems, assassins, loan sharks, predatory businessmen, and other merchants right off the bat. Not that all of the above creates harmony and well-being. Still, instead of fantasizing and absorbing ideas that destroy individualism and free trade we envision an exciting future in the mold of Star Wars: an active massive society held together by free trade, and a galactic army for self-defense. Although, it would be nice if we didn't need a military.

Before we move on, I would like to remind you that you not only possess the The Dynamic Rational Selfishness Weapon, you are the Dynamic Weapon.

The Rationally Selfish Individual sees through the data and discovers the truth of the situation; regardless of what it may uncover. He applies correct economic theories in his analysis. Praxeology, the science of human action soars as the "Real McCoy" in the field of economics. Here's a science that begins its analysis with individual actions. Isn't that exciting. You are an individual, so the real economics concerns you.

Social Altruists, Socialism and the Queen Bee

In the future, I hope we have a weak state, like in episodes 1 & 2 in Star Wars, rather than the terrible communistic feel of the human-apartheid applied future where they meddle with the affairs all around them; despite being told not do that. That my friend is the communist/socialist future we want to avoid. You must realize that socialists, Social Altruists and authoritarians hold it as a dream. Social Altruists only exist to change the lives of anyone around them. These misery-mongers want to shape you in the image of their spurious values and morals. Time to Ready, Aim, Fire. It doesn't matter what you want. You're just another worker bee, storing honey for the Queen Bee. Of course, the Social Altruist sees himself as the Queen Bee. You conquer one of life's illusions when you see through a Social Altruist. You discover that he holds no values that enhance human life; he's the epitome of anti-life. Your Dynamic Weapons are meant to preserve and enhance life.

We should hope for a future run on markets and money. The ability to own your time, make something and then be able to sell it is a fundamental pillar/pathway to success. Under socialist states you don't own your time, what you produce, or even your precious life. The rights of the individual are trampled upon in the name of common good; while the people are demonized in media and social media. In a socialist system you have no choices, you don't even own your own life, and if you don't like it—tough shit. You can't leave. Let's say you decide you don't want to work. Well, they've got a camp for that. Outside of Social Altruists who seek power, only ivory tower intellectual goofballs endorse socialism. Do I have to tell you where your Dynamic Weapons are needed.

Do we need a government or not? As much as I like the ideas put forth by Anarcho-Capitalists, I believe we need a extremely small government that only protects the individual's life, liberty and property. You know it would be nice if Anarcho-Capitalists could prove me wrong.

Government, Social Altruists and Markets

Once you've become painfully aware of the depth of intrusive and counter-productive government market interventions it is harder and harder for you to to defend them. Our government runs economic policy through any means it can centralize. It props up its dogma in an attempt to make it invincible from your critique and analysis. It is quite ironic that the government tries to run our economic policy as a nation or as a world in an environment that is the opposite of a meritocracy. Markets are amazing at self-assembling and self-replicating. After all, they are made up of you, me and everyone else. Markets will always find a way because they are similar to life. Let's go one step further and state "Markets are life."

It is almost as if our government wishes to change the rules and results for social evolution. Base evolution means only the strongest survive. Fortunately, unhampered capitalism guarantees the survival of those who may have physical and mental limitations. When Social Altruists hamper market processes, these debaucherers guarantee the weak, but potentially productive members of society will perish. And you wonder why Social Altruists actually manifest as anti-life. Well, the Rationally Selfish Individual thrives as an individual who loves life. He's always armed with the Dynamic Unhampered Capitalism Weapon.

The population on our planet has multiplied. Tragically, adverse circumstances wiped many ethnic groups and cultures off the face of the map. Because they went extinct and stopped spreading their genetic code, we will never see or experience their tales, songs and history.

Unhampered capitalism guarantees that markets work according to consumer desires. That's right, your desires and ambitions matter. Government interventionism sabotages your ability to satisfy your most urgent needs. For instance, bailouts and other monetary schemes such as QE and ZIRP prevent us from learning lessons that could change the face of the modern economy. Instead, Fed policy drives us to follow their Keynesian quackery. We speed after illusory bubbles in hope of improving our financial well-being. However, the day arrives when the bubbles burst leaving us holding a bag of nothing but heartaches and empty promises.

The Rationally Selfish Individual doesn't chase the illusions of Social Altruists and monetary quacks. He uses his Dynamic Weapon of Rational Selfishness to conquer their illusions. In addition, he possesses the Dynamic Unhampered Capitalism Weapon to complete the job. Isn't conquering life's illusions exciting and rewarding.

Every bubble ends up benefiting a very select few of insiders. The privileged few profit by dumping the risk on members of the middle and lower class. You certainly don't want to known as a "schmuck" who got caught holding the bag. Conquering your illusions means you relinquish that embarrassing role.

You've heard of insider trading. It appears that at the top of the Executive, Legislative and Judicial branches insider trading is not illegal. Now, members of the establishment want to look like they are tough on white collar crime so they make sure that someone who has fallen out of favor with the establishment gets arrested, tried and convicted of insider trading. Gee, I wonder what Martha Stewart did to take the role of a scapegoat.

Unhampered capitalism takes the heat for the creation of a class of 1,000 inside traders. So people start believing that it must be controlled. Now that's similar to gun control arguments. You know the gun commits the crime. Soon all kinds of socialists and Marxists arrive on the scene presenting spurious social and economic solutions that if instituted would cause a social collapse. It's an illusion to blame capitalism when it's anti-capitalism causing our social and economic problems. You must accept the unhappy fact that Social Altruists want to take away your Dynamic Unhampered Capitalism Weapon. Fortunately, you exist as the Dynamic Rational Selfishness Weapon. You use the ammo of logic and reason to blow away floating abstractions and illusions.

We've seen bailouts, market liquidity injections(QE) and inflation which resulted in a Consumer Purchasing Power Parity decrease for the American people. The dollar may currently appear strong (by the time you read this it might be showing long-term foundational weakness) but once it weakens anyone who is unlucky enough to find their currencies directly tied to it could start to grow a grudge. In addition, once people find it difficult to purchase the goods they need to survive, the negative emotions of hate, anger and envy begin to surface. Obviously, we're at the mercy of cronyism, nepotism, and plain old ineptitude and incompetence. It wasn't always like this. Social Altruists, do-gooders and world-improvers hurt people in the name of the "common good." Well, we see through their illusions—and we possess Dynamic Weapons and an abundance of ammo. Bye bye Social Altruism and irrational selfishness; hello Rational Selfishness. You are the Dynamic Weapon and the possessor of it. You soar as the conquering hero. You slay one illusion after another.

Social Altruists manifest as megalomaniacs, who believe they possess the ability to solve everyone's problems. We've seen that these sociopaths lack the mental and emotional maturity to look at circumstances from the point of view of the lone individual. That's why their social schemes end up causing the collapse of economic systems. Aggregates don't act; but individuals like you and me act to improve our well-being. The Social Altruist cares nothing for you as a unique human being. You're just fodder for his deadly illusions. You already know the art of self-defense. Ready, Aim, Fire.

Social Programs - The Lack of Accountability

Social programs lack accountability (rational profit and loss analysis) because they're bureaucratic endeavors. How do you fix a social program that fails miserably? You throw more of the taxpayers money after it. Lack of accountability means that money (your money) disappears down a bureaucratic rat hole.

The accountability problem exposes one of the main things wrong with the American government and other governments worldwide. Society's problems are "reserved" for bratty socialites and ivory tower intellectuals who studied at establishment colleges. I just introduced you to people who completely divorce themselves from reality. We might as well hire witch doctors to cure what ails our economy. Wait a minute. Don't bother. They're already here. It's time to get your battle gear ready.

We're saddled with a sick system where we expect large corporate like non-government organizations (non-profit) with no accountability, oversight, analysis, or transparency to solve problems. That's an illusion you must conquer. Many non-profit organizations have proved to be scams. How about the less than Snow White existence of The Breast Cancer Charity, Lance Armstrong's Live Strong and even the Wounded Warrior Project. Tragically, non-profit organizations often commit massive financial crimes.

I am willing to state that quite often (not always) people in non-profit organizations usually tend to be much worse than anyone you would ever meet on Wall Street. How can that be? Non-profit organizations attract Social Altruists. Need I say more.

Think, Feel and Act the Social Altruist's Way

After the American Gilded Age and the victory in World War 1 (if we could call it that) people *felt* that we owed it to each other and society to create a wealth of social systems and services, many of which are collapsing or have already collapsed. Would you like to think, feel and act as a Social Altruist thinks, feels and act? Here's how you accomplish that "astonishing" feat. You make sure your argument lacks all theoretical foundations, and that it completely disregards empirical facts and data. You justify anything you want to do by grabbing floating abstractions from the ether and backing them with strong emotions and feelings. You also make sure logic and reason don't enter the picture. That's what you call a disarmament package.

Let me put it to you straight. Even though your positive emotions can supply you much pleasure, they are not tools of cognition. You act as a Social Altruist when you abandon logic and reason by resorting to negative emotions and feelings. Your feelings might greatly influence the goods and services you choose to buy or not buy. Excellent sales people know that something is often bought with emotion, then justified with logic. However, don't make the mistake of believing your feelings control markets.

Conquering life's illusions means that you understand that cold-hearted consumers care nothing for your feelings. When a person satisfies his needs on the marketplace, he doesn't consider whether or not he's hurting your feelings or causing you other discomfort. The fact that you need a sale remains irrelevant to a consumer satisfying his most urgent desires. If he happens to throw an undeserved sale your way consider it charity. It won't be enough to save your business or job.

Nobody should be punished for having feelings, but if you decide to lobby and solicit massive social change based on how you feel or how someone made you feel, you abandoned your role as a Rationally Selfish Individual. Feelings based illogic leads the way to the tyranny of Social

Altruists, do-gooders and world-improvers. Who needs this reactionary BS. You, the Rationally Selfish Individual possesses enough Dynamic Weapons to explode the bull.

Social Altruists create a giving persona in order to trick people into supporting them. At the start, some righteously believe what they do will actually benefit people. The heck with the reality that they can only accomplish their goals by taking from Peter to give to Paul. If a Social Altruist feels something is right, he will completely ignore the laws of human action (economics). In fact, he denies they even exist. To him, anything goes in the field of economics. The only scientific studies he endorses are those pseudo-reports that back up his feelings and unfocused thoughts. Whether he admits or not he is a wolf dressed in sheep's clothing. You must recognize a Social Altruist when you see one. Failure to use your Dynamic Weapons in a timely manner could result in the loss of your personal liberty and economic freedom.

Social Altruists Love Victims

Social Altruists just "love" victims. These purveyors of human anguish offer "services" that result in their victims residing in a "sick house of pawns." They use their victims as pawns in order to capture other victims, which of course cements their power and prestige. Gathering up an enormous amount of victims creates a sorrowful group of misfits I call a Mobocracy. I'm sure you get the point. I hope you have plenty of ammo stashed.

You must accept the fact the Social Altruist cares nothing for the individual. He especially despises the Rationally Selfish Individual. A man (woman) who lives for his own sake will never play the role of a victim. You will stand up to a Social Altruist. You're always prepared to Ready, Aim, Fire. Are you beginning to see why you should embrace your Dynamic Weapons as best friends.

Do you realize that Social Altruism brought us people like Adolf Hitler, Mussolini, Lenin and Hillary Clinton? It gives us bloated budgets, Central Banking, government interventionism, socialism, the bloodshed of wars and all the other anti-social schemes that destroy personal liberty and economic freedom. Your Dynamic Weapons are honorable and just. You use them to free people from the oppression of personal, social and economic illusions.

The Social Altruist Mutates Into a Social Nihilist

You've heard the old medical adage, "first do no harm." That doesn't apply to sociopaths and psychopaths who manifest as Social Nihilists. Social Altruists often carry some of the traits of the irrationally selfish. You know that's a deadly combination. It's time to get your Dynamic Weapons ready for action.

Social Nihilists don't care about anything or anybody. They're full-blooded psychopaths. They're irrationally selfish, greedy, and will do whatever they want to to get ahead. Since they come from the same "litter" as Social Altruists they can effectively play the part of a do-gooder or world-improver. Here's the type of person who easily creates concentration camps and gas chambers. On the other hand, if he loses, he quite readily moves on to his next project of mass extermination, unless he's permanently stopped. You will seldom meet a Social Nihilist in everyday life. If you do run into him your Dynamic Weapons will protect you. However, you don't want to live in a country he's taken over. He will make sure the "gestapo" completely disarms you. As you're marched to the death house, you'll wonder why you didn't use your Dynamic Rational Selfishness Weapon to escape the premises. Once a Social Altruist mutates into a Social Nihilist and takes over a country, you can expect human degradation, poverty and mass murder to run amuck.

Social Altruists, Marriage and Family

Another way Social Altruists attempt to create demographical and societal collapse is through the progressive tax system. One of the most destructive tax remains the marriage penalty. You should realize that these bird-brained "progressives" do everything possible to blur the distinction between the sexes and destroy the traditional marriage. Their wicked welfare schemes guarantee unwed mothers raise children who suffer the handicap of no male guidance. It actually pays for the mother not to know who the father is—or at least pretend not to know. That's what you call a short-term mentality. You realize that Social Altruists just love victims. Can you imagine how many children will grow to adulthood severely damaged, lacking the necessary tools to succeed in everyday life.

Why would Social Altruists downplay the importance of masculinity. One horrible reason is that they want to institute the State as the great Father Figure. Unfortunately, it's worse than that. Eventually the Father Figure gives way to the great Mother Figure. The wicked bastards want to feminize society. It's time to ready your Dynamic Weapons for immediate use. Ready, Aim, Fire and Fire again.

If our society runs completely on the female principle, it makes you wonder where the children will come from. Even a country that's hampered with stupid economic policies such as France realizes that you need to have children in order to keep the state going; and even the Franks incentivize marriage and children.

Something just occurred to me. If Social Altruists completely feminize our society and succeed in eliminating marriage, artificial insemination could "solve" the problem. Virile males could be used as sperm slaves. It's time to ready all of your Dynamic Weapons and attack.

By the way, don't get me wrong. I love women. I would like to see all individuals reach his or her full potential. Still, the fact remains that men are men and women are women. It takes a reality evading, power seeking Social Altruist to deny biological facts.

In America we don't have hardly anyone from the political arena brave enough to oppose Social Altruists. Most Republicans exist as "wet noodles", always caving in to the demands of modern progressives. The Mainstream Press attempts to eviscerate anyone with enough courage to oppose destructive BS. As a Rationally Selfish Individual you know what you are up against. The opposition uses the weapons of illogic, unreason, hate and envy to attack individual rights. Social Altruists attempt to disarm you before the battle even begins with their politically correct crap. You know what to do. Ready, Aim, Fire. The fact that they ignore the deadly effectiveness of the Dynamic Unhampered Capitalism Weapon supplies you a distinct advantage. Sometimes its easy to deny something you fear. You can effectively take advantage of their denials and illusions.

You, the Rationally Selfish Individual, realize that unhampered capitalism and individual rights will lead to world peace and economic prosperity faster than any other method. Imagine a world where the individual no longer has to worry about Social Altruists violating his personal liberty and economic freedom. Let's go one step further an visualize a community of Rationally Selfish Individuals trading value for value. How rewarding! However, until then you must be ready to use all of your Dynamic Weapons.

One more incentive exists for you to throw your complete support behind the social system of unhampered capitalism—children. You may or may not have children. Regardless they offer hope for the future. Wouldn't it be wonderful for them to seize the opportunities you didn't have. How about the possibility of a young boy or girl growing up and living life to its fullest. It's exciting that a rewarding existence that includes happiness and success became a reality because your Dynamic Weapons finally defeated the wicked Social Altruists and their deadly social and economic schemes.

Make sure that your children's existence is firmly rooted in reality. Allowing them to enjoy some fantasy stimulates their imagination. However, the Easter Bunny, Santa Claus and Tooth Fairy myths won't carry them through reality. There will come a day when they must relinquish the philosophy behind these myths forever. Eventually you will have to arm them with the Dynamic Weapons you successfully use.

Whatever you do, don't set them up for false success. If you raise a child to think, feel and act as the Rationally Selfish Individual thinks, feels and acts, you won't have to worry about Social Altruists getting hold of his (her) body, mind and spirit. If you default on your basic duty as a parent, don't be shocked when the politically correct BS captures his mind, turns it off and converts him to an unfocused feeling machine. Do you think Social Altruists make good parents? All you have to do is look at the decay in our society for the answer.

Your children will experience some doubt and confusion, but with your guidance they will successfully move through the minefield of illusions, arriving at a destination called personal liberty and economic freedom. You will have raised Rationally Selfish Individuals.

Conclusion

If you are painfully aware that all government intervention on the marketplace is counter-productive and downright destructive—if you have decided that Social Altruism and irrational selfishness is not in your best interest—if you realize the rationally selfish life is the one for you, then you have no choice but to support the only system that is rational and logical—unhampered capitalism.

Here's one more incentive for supporting unhampered capitalism (free enterprise). If you have children and you want them to have the chance to seek new opportunities and to live a life of happiness and success—you must wholeheartedly embrace the social system of unhampered capitalism. Someday your children's children's children may thank you and their lucky stars.

Even though they're in denial, Social Altruists subconsciously fear the Dynamic Unhampered Capitalism Weapon because it would permanently put them out of their misery. In the next chapter, I will discuss the next Dynamic Weapon the Rationally Selfish Individual, the impeccable warrior must possess to guarantee his success and happiness.

The Rationally Selfish Individual possesses spiritual blessings such as self-reliance, love of values and respect for his fellow man's life, liberty and property. He will effectively use his Dynamic Weapons to defend individual rights.

CHAPTER FIVE

DYNAMIC MIND POWER WEAPON

It's common for the individual to think that he embraces the life-enhancing philosophy of Rational Selfishness, but then somehow he fails to exercise control over his thoughts, feelings and actions. An unpleasant series of circumstances throws him into a situation that results in a sudden lack of self-control. Suddenly, he (she) reveals the irrational selfishness that's been lurking in the background by lashing out at others or indulging in some self-defeating activities. If something similar happens to you don't worry. It's happened to us all. You can conquer it with your new Dynamic Mind Power Weapon. Mind Power allows you to use your Dynamic Weapons with deadly effectiveness. You will also notice that we begin integrating your Dynamic Weapons into a psychological arsenal of attack and self-defense.

Remember what we discovered about guilt. You can't beat yourself up because you occasionally fail. You must accept the fact that the pursuit of Rational Selfishness continues as a lifetime endeavor. The idea is to get better and better, day in and day out. Although we believe in individualism and self-reliance, nobody completely escapes the ravages of society's illusions. In our misguided society, we glorify irrational selfishness by placing incentives for people to act mean and nasty. Often the bully receives the loudest and longest applause. If you've spend some time in our public school system, you know the unpleasant consequences of coming in contact with bullies.

We proved that sitting tight and following the rules guarantees you play the role of sacrificial victim. That's why we first supplied you the Dynamic Anti-Social Altruism Weapon. Although the Social Altruist acts like he presents people a loving, giving philosophy of life, he actually incentivizes people to act as nasty as possible and to use nastiness in legally and psychologically violent ways that would have been frowned on in previous generations. Fortunately, you are building a psychological arsenal of attack and self-defense.

Since you exist as a Rationally Selfish Individual, you must recognize and understand the dangerous slippery road you're walking on. Long held thoughts and beliefs that don't serve you place roadblocks in your path. Your own illusions offer you the most difficult challenges. The Dynamic Rational Selfishness Weapon provides you power and direction. However, you must learn to use it effectively. In addition, the rest of your arsenal of Dynamic Weapons guarantees you conquer a variety of deadly illusions.

Your personality, mentality, attitude and ethics stand at the forefront, creating your life. Some of these traits reside in your subconscious mind. You consciously desire to adopt the role of the Rationally Selfish Individual. Your subconscious mind says no, we're not going in that direction. You suffer the frustration of failure. Fortunately, for you along comes the Dynamic Mind Power Weapon. The Rationally Selfish Individual uses it wisely. You must remember that you not only possess the Dynamic Rational Selfishness Weapon, you escalate as the weapon. The Dynamic Weapon fires the Dynamic Weapons. That's what we call personal power.

The Rationally Selfish Individual supports free speech. Still, do you often lose your bearings, becoming overly emotionally when someone tells you something that pushes your buttons? I understand that Social Altruists and irrationally selfish people assault you with propaganda, lies and half-truths. Regardless, you must continue to support their right to say just about anything they want to say. You have a choice. You can attempt to refute them or you can walk away, refusing to waste your time dealing with nonsense. You TAKE CHARGE of your thoughts, feelings and actions. That's Mind Power. You can see where the name of your latest Dynamic Weapon came from.

Unpleasant circumstances appear rather undesirable. They can make you or break you. Have you considered the possibility that they serve as a test of your ability to handle adversity? I know. You're thinking "Who need this industrial strength BS." You have a choice. You can act like the majority of people and accept the role of a loser or you can grab the unpleasant circumstances by the horns, take control and emerge as a true winner. You know how the Rationally Selfish Individual handles life's challenges.

Your thoughts control your emotions and feelings, which in turn controls your attitude. Your attitude can make a big difference in determining whether your journey is happy or unhappy. I suggest you TAKE CHARGE of your attitude by taking control of your thoughts. When you have a negative thought, replace it with its opposite. Have you ever counted all the self-sabotaging thoughts that pop into your mind? You might be shocked when you see the final count. The Rationally Selfish Individual will not allow garbage thoughts to destroy his goals and desires. He pulls out his Dynamic Mind Power Weapon and begins eradicating them.

When you mentally and emotionally separate from the flock/mob you grow as a person. The Rationally Selfish Individual doesn't attempt to manipulate people's feelings. That seldom ends well, because alienating worthy people doesn't lead to social success. Even worse, you might turn off someone who desires to trade value for value, depriving yourself of a successful personal or business relationship.

What you do or don't do determines whether you win or lose. You're at the mercy of cause and effect relationships. Action leads to results; however the actions you embark upon have to be grounded in reality. The irrationally selfish individual bounces here and there in a world of illusion, ending up in sorrowful places that winners avoid. You use your Dynamic Weapons to conquer illusions.

Conquering Second-Handed Living

The Rationally Selfish Individual holds nothing but contempt for second-handed living. Ayn Rand states *"A second-hander is one who regards the consciousness of other men as superior to his own and to the facts of reality. It is to a second-hander that the moral appraisal of himself by others is a primary concern which supersedes truth, facts, reason, logic. The disapproval of others is so shatteringly terrifying to him that nothing can withstand its impact within his consciousness; thus he would deny the evidence of his own eyes and invalidate his own consciousness for the sake of any stray charlatan's moral sanction. It is only a second-hander who could conceive of such absurdity as hoping to win an intellectual argument by hinting: "But people won't like you!"* When you start feeling like a second-hander, its time to get out your Dynamic Mind Power

Weapon. Ready, Aim, Fire.

You can act like your second-handed peers, and continue to remain a zero, or you can get on board the train to a powerful future. Your feelings and emotions will often betray you. Fortunately, the Rationally Selfish Individual knows when to listen to his heart. Later you will learn how to activate you intuitive powers. **Word of Warning**. Don't allow your emotions to contradict reason. I know that in affairs of the heart, this presents difficulties. When your emotions begin to soar, it's easy to send reason on an extended vacation. Don't ever leave home without your Dynamic Anti-Irrational Selfishness Weapon or your Dynamic Rational Selfishness Weapon. Remember you exist as a Dynamic Weapon using your Dynamic Weapons. It's rather embarrassing wandering around naked.

The Rationally Selfish Individual discovers what works and doesn't work. The journey always remains challenging and even the most effective individuals make mistakes. The idea is to keep the mishaps to a minimum and to avoid making the Big Mistake, which is often fatal. I guarantee that if you start thinking effectively and positively—and you begin eliminating negative thoughts, you will permanently alter your life in ways you can't even fathom right now. As a Rationally Selfish Individual, you shape your destiny with the Dynamic Mind Power Weapon.

Economic Hardship + Irrational Selfishness = Negative Emotions

Whether you like it or not, personal and economic hardships show you your true colors. Do you display the bleached out colors of defeat and despair or do you gloriously shine the rainbow colors of perseverance, success and love of values? Economic hardships affect people at the middle and bottom of the income scale. These groups find it difficult to keep bouncing back from the Fed's boom and bust cycles. Many of their dreams and desires are nothing more than bursting bubbles, courtesy of members of the political and financial establishment.

It's possible that an economic crisis will negatively effect a

8 Dynamic Weapons for Conquering Life's Illusions

Rationally Selfish Individual. Now here's where your Dynamic Weapons come in handy, especially your Mind Power Weapon. People begin unleashing the negative emotions of envy, jealousy and hate. These could very surface from your subconscious mind. For instance, siblings will be jealous and envious of other siblings who fared better when the bubbles began to burst. They will fall under the illusion that they deserve the money and property the more successful sibling possesses. It gets worse than that. The jealous brothers and sisters begin believing the successful sibling doesn't deserve to keep anything he or she owns. It takes 3 Dynamic Weapons to repel the viciousness of the attack. Time to rely on the Rational Selfishness, Anti-Irrational Selfishness and Mind Power Weapons. If people infested with hatred, envy and jealousy enlist the help of a Social Altruist, you know what other Dynamic Weapon you will need. Ready, Aim, Fire. It's time to eliminate "basket cases" from your life. You don't need irrationally selfish people dragging you down.

The envious person makes his unwanted appearance and constantly complains about what others have versus what he has. He(she) takes very little personal responsibility for the actions that brought him to the spot he's in. Envious thoughts surface from his subconscious, flooding his conscious mind with the anticipation of consequences *that haven't yet happened*. Incredibly, he uses negative thoughts to create his unhappy environment. What type of individual pollutes his life with with envy, jealousy and hatred? You know the answer to that question. It's the irrationally selfish person.

The envious person see everything "through a glass darkly." Since his persona is deeply rooted in irrational selfishness, achieving and working for what others have remains beyond him. If you have the "balls" to hit him with the truth by pointing out his sloth and laziness expect him to explode in anger. Here's a confrontation you don't need. Sometimes it's best to shelve your Dynamic Weapons and retreat. You're not actively seeking irrationally selfish people to confront. It's wise to avoid them when possible. If you find yourself in a situation where you must face one, you know what to do. Always be prepared to defend yourself against the onslaught of your enemies.

Is it easier to deal with an envious person than a jealous person? That's like asking if death by electricity is preferable to death by gassing.

Envy and jealousy come from the same litter of irrational selfishness.

Irrational Selfishness and Anger

    You know irrational selfishness has you lock, stock and barrel when you allow anger to control you. Here's where your Dynamic Mind Power Weapon comes in handy. I admit that in my years of immaturity I allowed anger to take control of my thoughts, feelings and actions. You couldn't exactly refer to me as an impeccable warrior. I'm still appalled at some of the words that spewed forth from my mouth. Not surprisingly, I also indulged in some irrationally selfish activities. Finally I made the the transformation to a Rationally Selfish Individual. Of course, I'm not perfect. Who is. In Chapter Seven, I will introduce you to a Dynamic Weapon that will help you quite a bit. It complements the Mind Power Weapon rather nicely. By the way, all the Dynamic Weapons complement each other. You are building a powerful psychological arsenal of attack and self defense.

    Anger has it uses in dangerous situations that threaten your very existence. It is a tool of survival. That's not what we're concerned with here. I am talking about the kind of anger that sabotages your relationships and peace of mind. Extreme, uncontrollable anger could land you in prison. That's not the ideal environment to test the effectiveness of your Dynamic Weapons. You use them to protect and expand your personal liberty and economic freedom. You definitely won't be taking these precious gifts to the penitentiary.

    During harsh economic conditions, we may all feel some anger about how the government and Federal Reserve System destroyed our wealth along with our most cherished values. Obviously, members of the elite cheated us. The Rationally Selfish Person doesn't go off half-cocked in a violent rage. He (She) knows his Dynamic Weapons will help him overcome adversity. He TAKES CHARGE of his thoughts, feelings and actions.

    The angry, irrationally selfish person feels cheated whether times are good or times are bad. His self-consuming behavior can become contagious. If you allow it, he will infect you by draining your positive emotions. His brain chemistry has spiraled so far out of whack, that his explosions often help him sleep better—at least in the short-term. When confronted by an angry person, you pause for a second, then you pull out your Dynamic Mind Power Weapon. Here's a weapon with many uses, which includes allowing you to walk way before anger inflicts damage on you. It effectively protects you from his anger and your potential angry response.

Parents and other authority figures often victimize children. This is especially damaging during their formal development years, somewhere between the ages of 3 and 7. You can see how a victim could develop into an angry person. Incidentally, some victims end up becoming severely depressed people. Here's an unfortunate person who lacks the oomph to act aggressively, except in a passive way. Anyway, a man or woman's internal seething eventually finds outward expression, much to everyone's detriment. If the irrationally selfish angry person also possesses sociopath or psychopathic tendencies he could attempt to "fix" society as a Social Altruist or just plain turn into a monster and run rampant over people's individual rights.

Let's say a sticky situation allows your anger to surface. In some cases, you have a good reason to be angry. The irrationally selfish person goes off half-cocked alienating people and inviting resistance. You can see that that's not very effective behavior. Powerful and productive people prefer not to deal with neurotic men and women. In addition, he depletes his positive energy. By now, you should know that abandoning your Dynamic Weapons of Anti-Irrational Selfishness and Rational Selfishness leads to destructive behavior patterns. You should also see how the Dynamic Mind Power Weapon reinforces all of your Dynamic Weapons.

The Rationally Selfish Individual controls his anger by not reacting at all or by forcefully stating his displeasure in a controlled manner. The impeccable warrior displays power in his actions. People take him seriously. You gain incredible power when you realize you not only possess the Dynamic Rational Selfishness Weapon, but you thrive as the Dynamic Weapon.

Irrational Selfishness and Hate

Hate and anger go round and round in a vicious circle game. You almost have to feel sorry for irrationally selfish people. They're on one of those circus merry-go-rounds that never stop. We can say they're captured by a carousel of illusion. Fortunately, you and I know how to jump off the sinister ride of never ending misery.

Neurotic authority figures instill hate in precious, young minds. When the child suffers a deep, frightening experience that ties in with the negative programming, a festering hate begins to pollute his subconscious mind. You never know what will cause it to surface. It's possible you grew up in an environment of race hatred. Grouping people won't cut the mustard. The Rationally Selfish Person judges each person as a unique individual. Sadly, we have Social Altruists using the race card (these parasites thrive on racism) and other unsavory social schemes in an attempt to consolidate their power. You know what Dynamic Weapon to use. Ready, Aim, Fire.

Irrational selfishness and hate make an unholy marriage. Although life presents you with predators you must repel, the hateful individual begins creating imaginary enemies. Social Altruists make hating with a passion easier by supplying irrationally selfish people with scapegoats. They just love victims—and when people walk around blinded by hatred—oppression, discriminatory rulings and prejudiced decisions wait around the corner to ambush innocent people.

Rationally Selfish and irrationally selfish people dislike the government for different reasons. We know that modern governments are good at starting wars, destroying economies, debauching currencies and violating individual rights. Social Altruists and irrationally selfish people run the show for an elite aristocracy that's hard to define. Rationally Selfish Individuals use their Dynamic Weapons to fight the cronyism and elitism of government interventionism. Irrationally selfish hateful people might consider firebombing institutions, not caring how many innocent people die. You've seen the results of fanaticism in action. Often, religious crusades attract these type of people.

Hate manifests as a very strong emotion, and it is driven by intense feelings and memories. The Rationally Selfish Individual avoids people who exhibit hate whenever possible. Should you be confronted with hate you have your Dynamic Weapons to protect you. If hate suddenly surfaces in your own mind, the Dynamic Mind Power Weapon will help you overcome it. As mentioned, in Chapter Seven we supply you a complementary weapon to conquer your negative emotions and subconscious illusions.

Do you want hateful people in your circle of friends? You should know by now that hate and irrational selfishness go together like gluttony and bloated bodies go together. Of course, if you receive some perverse thrill from abandoning your Dynamic Anti-Irrational Selfishness Weapon-------------. By the way, you don't need to act vengeful and full of wrath to indulge in hatred. Some people commit a slow suicide by directing it inward. You can imagine their fate when they also indulge in some other irrationally selfish activities.

Irrational Selfishness, Hate and Revenge

People infested with hate lack a full understanding of their motives and the situations they find themselves in. These unfortunate individuals sink to the bottom of the negative emotion pit. A Rationally Selfish Person should know better than to allow an argumentative, hateful man or woman to drag him into an abyss of no return. Have you ever attempted to win an argument with an irrationally selfish evader of reality? It can't be done because logic and reason isn't part of his repertoire of argumentative tools. Before I discovered the Dynamic Mind Power Weapon, I allowed Mr. and Mrs. Emotional Basket Case to drive me crazy. When Easter arrived, we would share the same basket of tooth-decaying delights. You can imagine how the Easter Egg Hunt went. Red was green and blue was yellow. The purple eggs were off limit, even though they were actually orange. When bedtime arrived, I began counting Easter bunnies in order to go to sleep. I'm sure you get point. Associating with irrationally selfish people on a regular basis can turn you into a basket case.

In his bestselling book "Looking Out for Number #1" Robert Ringer offers us the "I'm Crazy, You're Sane Theory." *"If you allow a relationship with a neurotic individual to continue for too long, you run the risk of his convincing you that he is perfectly sane and that you are the one who's crazy."*

Who is responsible for your life? Irrationally selfish people refuse to take responsibility for their lives. When things go wrong it's always the fault of somebody else. The blame game leads to hatred and intolerance because it violates the laws of reality. You must realize that other people are not necessarily responsible for everything that has happened to you. Since men and women share similar frustrations and disappointments in life, they can be quite sympathetic to your trials and tribulations.

Joe Vitale says *"Total responsibility for my life means that everything in my life—simply because it is in my life—is my responsibility. In a literal sense, the entire world is my creation."* Now that's profound wisdom the Rationally Selfish Individual can live by.

Are you under the illusion that people like people who hate people? Only a masochist or a Social Altruist becomes enamored with a hateful man or woman. Some irrationally selfish people might hang around him or her for "protection" or the "thrill" of indulging in self-defeating activities. Neurotic people feed on each other in a vicious cycle of self-sabotage. When a group of hateful people get together for one of their nefarious causes the mob mentality takes over. It's time to get your Dynamic Weapons ready. You may need your whole psychological arsenal of attack and self-defense. Ready, Aim, Fire and Fire more ammo. On the other hand, an extended vacation to distant planet could provide you a viable solution to a Mobocracy. Even the Rationally Selfish Person can occasionally fantasize. Let's get back to reality.

Do you remember the movie "The Blob." The sci-fi classic follows teenagers Steve (Steven McQueen) and his best girl, Jane (Aneta Corseaut), as they try to protect their hometown from a gelatinous alien life form that engulfs everything it touches. Well, that could very well describe hatred. Hatred is a malignant force that can grow larger and larger. Something bad happens to an irrationally selfish person who unfortunately has hate lurking in the background. It takes over his thoughts, feelings and actions. The next thing you know more bad stuff occurs. His hate continues to expand until it's all consuming. Since he doesn't recognize a feedback loop, even if it is delivered to his front door in a impressive package with a colorful bow, he begins descending into a hell on earth. Anyone around him gets to take the trip with him, unless of course, he or she possesses a few appropriate Dynamic Weapons.

When things go wrong as they often do, the irrationally selfish person fails to see the real reason for the failure and frustration. Instead of looking within, he or she looks outward for the cause of the problems. I admit that members of the political and financial establishment do everything in their power to screw us over. That's one reason I'm supplying you with Dynamic Weapons. However, the Rationally Selfish Individual develops the ability to look within because that's where the solutions often reside. How do you successfully look within? Stay tuned for Chapter Seven. I'm happy to say that an exciting Dynamic Weapon awaits you.

You can see that hatred becomes further and further entrenched, spiraling into a Shakespearean self-tragedy. We end up with the tragic result of hatred and anger combining in a terrible way that leads from hurtful thoughts to hurtful and regrettable actions.

When an irrationally selfish person firmly believes something is unfair, he lashes out at other people with angry, hurtful words. When he finally loses his mind and begins running amuck, he jumps into the revenge mode. The Rationally Selfish Individual might believe that success is the best revenge. I don't blame you if you want to savor your moment of revenge. Using your Dynamic Weapons to conquer your enemies brings you enormous rewards. When the irrationally selfish man or woman hopelessly loses his or her cool—jealousy, envy, hate and anger manifest together in actual actions and behaviors well beyond the thought threshold. You've heard the saying "Hell has no fury like a woman scorned." We should revise it say "Hell has no fury like an irrationally selfish woman scorned." Some men give into murderous impulses when events take them beyond their threshold of what they can handle. Douglas Horton said *"When seeking revenge, dig two graves, one for yourself."* You can see why you want to live your life as the Dynamic Rational Selfishness Weapon.

Have you ever considered the consequences of giving into hate and anger and resorting to revenge? You might think that what you are doing is righteous and justified, but that isn't how you look to other people. The Rationally Selfish Individual will think you lost your mind.

Pure and simple, unbridled revenge can cause immense hurt and damage to another person. You don't need the legal ramifications of your date in civil or criminal court.

Some hateful, irrationally selfish men and women actually get high off the drug of revenge. When they lash out at others their brain chemistry receives an adrenaline rush resulting in momentary pleasure. Where's Dr. Sigmund Freud when you need him? He wisely stated *"Civilized society is perpetually menaced with disintegration through this primary hostility of men towards one another."*

As a Rationally Selfish Individual you want to attract the right people into your life. If your dealing from a deck of cards with the suits of envy, anger, hate and revenge, most people will see you as a villain, an irrationally selfish "card shark." Nobody in their right mind wants to play in a game rigged by negative emotions. In addition, when you act in revenge against someone, you trivialize their rights; including the right not to be violently molested and verbally or physically assaulted. It's difficult to gain anyone's sympathy when you use arbitrary grounds to declare war on someone. People will see you as a tyrant—and you know the bloody mess tyrants have created with their wars and oppression. Can you see how important your Dynamic Mind Power Weapon is? It allows you to use your other Dynamic Weapons much more effectively. Obviously your Dynamic Rational Selfishness Weapon remains your most important apparatus of attack and self-defense. Why? Because you not only use it to battle the enemies of personal liberty and economic freedom, you exist as the Dynamic Weapon.

How can you expect people to respect you when you wear the armor of a tyrant? Since you live as a Rationally Selfish Individual I'm confident you'll never adopt the persona of one. The good news is nearly every tyrant or would-be tyrant can be cooled off with constant action and a unique understanding of the world. Your Dynamic Weapons use the ammo of action and understanding.

The revengeful person says that his rights stand above the rights of the counter-party. When he pulls the trigger of his irrational weapons, he resorts to actions that the Rationally Selfish Person would never consider. When circumstances confront you with a situation that's meant to unleash your anger, you keep your cool. You understand that a carefully organized response will do more for you in any situation than committing a violent, spiteful action pushed forward by revenge. I hope you realize that your Dynamic Weapons protect and enhance your body, mind and spirit.

Irrational Selfishness and the Pursuit of Wealth

People alienated or disenfranchised from society often pursue wealth in order to show it off. Conspicuous displays of wealth in luxury items, luxury cars, big homes and even private jets raises their precarious self-worth and self-esteem. As you probably noticed we are referring to irrationally selfish people. The Rationally Selfish Individual might accumulate all the above in order to improve the quality of his life. However, he already possesses high self-worth. He (she) doesn't need to build up his self-esteem by showing off.

In the modern age people have pursued money and items of value more than any other society. Our society completely revolves around an illusory consumerism. As Rationally Selfish Individuals, we endorse people accumulating wealth in the free market. One of your Dynamic Weapons tells you that we wholeheartedly support unhampered capitalism. Unfortunately, the Fed's easy money policies along with the government's entitlement mentality spawned a covetousness that invades every aspect and element of the life of the average man and woman. Social Altruists created a monster of consumerism. On the other hand, these purveyors of economic mischief support policies that destroy the free enterprise system. Time to get out your Dynamic Anti-Social Altruism Weapon. Ready, Aim, Fire.

A greedy lawyer will encourage a woman to get married, then file for divorce with the goal of taking more than 50% of the poor guy's assets. I understand that in certain cases a woman may be entitled to a hefty settlement. Still, we have a legal system that favors divorce over marriage. How much money do lawyers make from divorce cases? I guess it could get worse. Some lawyers go into politics. Now, I'm not against all lawyers. Someday, you might need a highly competent attorney. Anyway, Perry Mason remains one of my favorite TV shows.

There are honest and dishonest ways to create wealth. Unhampered capitalism encourages men and women to make money through productive effort. Government interventionism or what some call crony capitalism guarantees some people gain wealth at the expense of others. We need to return to honesty and integrity—and as a society we must hold corporate criminals and bankers to the regular justice system just like anyone else. We exposed the establishment scams in Chapter Four and supplied you with the Dynamic Unhampered Capitalism Weapon.

Balance in life is the key to success and happiness. The Rationally Selfish Individual firmly believes in earning wealth by indulging in productive activities. He also knows that happiness results from balancing the needs of his body, mind and spirit. The Rationally Selfish Individual know that covetousness leads to unparalleled greed and malice towards people and markets. The irrationally selfish man or woman goes up and down on a seesaw of greed and frustration, experiencing short artificial highs and desperate lows. Exodus 20 of the Bible (King James Version) says the following about covetousness, one of The Ten Commandments. *"Thou shalt not covet thy neighbour's house, thou shalt not covet thy neighbour's wife, nor his manservant, nor his maidservant, nor his ox, nor his ass, nor any thing that is thy neighbour's."* Now that's some ammo you can use in your Dynamic Anti-Irrational Selfishness Weapon. Once again I remind you that you exist as the Dynamic Rational Selfishness Weapon.

Irrational Selfishness and Jealousy

The final emotion I want to touch on feasts at same banquet of despair as envy, defeat, self destruction, and suicide. The changing world disrupted economic systems and globalization forcing a lot of people to fundamentally re-think their lives. The Rationally Selfish Individual attempts to anticipate change and act accordingly. He analyzes his success and his failures in order to move in a happier more profitable direction. You must realize that even success oriented people run into blocks and obstacles, falling flat on their faces. Fortunately, these courageous individuals believed Norman Vincent Peale when he said *"Every problem has in it the seeds of its own solution. If you don't have any problems, you don't get any seeds."*

8 Dynamic Weapons for Conquering Life's Illusions

The irrationally selfish person indulges in short-term thinking and immediate gratification to the extreme. His self-defeating behavior results in personal and professional failure. He looks around and sees others doing much better than him. Since he's not perceptive enough to look in the mirror for the source of his problems, he begins looking outward. He discovers that there are no answers to be found. In his state of despair, he allows jealousy to take control of his very being. He (she) denies reality and shuns the teachings that could possibly help set him free. There's no reading Norman Vincent Peale's "The Power of Positive Thinking", Napoleon Hill's "Think and Grow Rich" or Robert Ringer's "Looking Out for #1" once your jealous mind begins to believe that you're the victim of a deep fundamental social injustice caused by your more successful rationally selfish peers.

If only the irrationally selfish person could discover the Dynamic Rational Selfishness Weapon and transform his whole being. As mentioned, jealousy feasts with envy at the same banquet of despair. Once jealousy seizes control of your thoughts, feelings and actions, you develop an uncontrollable urge for things you cannot have. You might enlist Social Altruists to confiscate them from hard-working successful people, but you will never feel good about it. The "Keeping up with the Jones'" mentality at all costs creates a hell on earth. The ancient Chinese had a quote that I believe is very applicable to what we've been discussing. *"Comparison disrupts cosmic harmony"* - Unknown. Do you think irrational selfishness and cosmic harmony go together?

Your Dynamic Weapons conquer personal and economic illusions. All negative emotions are born from illusion. By comparing yourself to everyone else and gauging your success based on the results of others, you reinforce the illusions that trap you in a life of failure and frustration. Although we haven't covered fear as a separate category, you must realize all negative emotions express an underlying fear of life. Wouldn't you rather live in love than in fear? The Rationally Selfish Individual loves his highest values. In 1 John 4:18 of King James Version of the Bible we discover that *"There is no fear in love; but perfect love casteth out fear: because fear hath torment. He that feareth is not made perfect in love."* The irrationally selfish person cannot love with all of his heart and soul because his negative emotions cast out real love.

Negative emotions can and will destroy personal relationships. Jealousy–the green-eyed monster of relationship destruction guarantees love will flee the scene. I wrote an article that explains what happens when lovers allow jealousy to destroy their relationship. Here's the link. http://libertarianway.me/2015/04/16/jealousy-the-green-eyed-monster-of-relationship-destruction/.

Imagine unjustly feeling that your more successful peers are morons who benefited from the injustice that runs rampant in our society. Yeah, they don't deserve all the good things they have. In a just society I would be on top of the heap. I wonder if changing the social structure might get the job done. Once irrationally selfish people begin falling off the edge of reason and rationality, tumbling into an abyss of jealousy, envy and covetousness, you need to protect your personal liberty and economic freedom—immediately. Time to reach for your Dynamic Anti-Irrational Selfishness Weapon. Ready, Aim, Fire. You will probably need your Dynamic Anti-Social Altruism Weapon once their allies the Social Altruists show up.

Once Again, Anger Arrives on the Scene

The irrationally selfish person invites failure and frustration into his life which causes anger to rear its ugly head. You're probably thinking "Oh no! Not anger again." Here's an emotion that causes you to lose your cool. It's particularly dangerous because it leads to actions contrary to others' basic human rights. Uncontrollable anger might give neurotic people an immediate rush of pleasure, but often it's the starting point for a visit to the penitentiary, not a very pleasurable place for an lengthy vacation. The Rationally Selfish Person avoids angers like he would avoid any self-defeating behavior. We can wonder if the irrationally selfish person receives the same rush from anger as the drug addict receives from crack cocaine.

The irrationally selfish individual becomes lost in a labyrinth of negative stereotypes and generalizations, which results in strong prejudices surfacing. The further removed from reality he becomes, the more he turns to hate and anger for temporary relief. He no longer sees each man and woman as a unique individual. He's unable to empathize with their struggles, their pain and sorrow. If a person somehow overcomes his trials and tribulations with success and happiness, the irrationally selfish person goes into his hate, anger, envy, jealousy mode. Maybe we should feel pity for someone who shed his basic humanity. Unfortunately, all you can do is get your Dynamic Weapons ready for action. And whatever you do, never leave home without your Dynamic Rational Selfishness Weapon. It's rather embarrassing to allow people to see you wandering around naked. Your Rationally Selfish friends and associates will think you joined the enemy.

You can see the irrationally selfish person as a snowball rolling down a steep decline to a warmer environment. He might think he's getting bigger and more powerful; however eventually he melts his life away through one illusion after another. He accelerates his demise when vengeful thoughts begin polluting his mind. Vigilantes rarely enjoy a happy and prosperous future. Their behavior involves various degrees of violence. Vigilantes may assault targets verbally, physically, vandalize property, or even kill individuals. Here's where anger has run amuck. First degree murder usually ends up with someone taking a trip to Death Row. Aren't you thankful that you exist as a Rationally Selfish Individual—and don't you feel grateful for possessing a psychological arsenal of Dynamic Weapons to conquer life's illusions.

Once an irrationally selfish individual loses his empathy for the honest people who make up a thriving society, he finds it's virtually impossible to bond with them. He becomes oblivious to the fact that once you create feelings of appreciation and gratitude, you attract into your life that which you can appreciate and feel gratitude for. The Rationally Selfish Individual possesses spiritual blessings such as self-reliance, love of values and respect for his fellow man's life, liberty and property. You now know that you can supply your Dynamic Weapons with the ammo of appreciation, gratitude, love and respect. Are you beginning to understand that your Dynamic Weapons enhance and preserve life? Social Altruists and irrationally selfish people resort to "weapons" that either diminish life or destroy it. Social Altruism sinks into the abyss as the anti-life philosophy of sacrifice—self-sacrifice and the sacrifice of innocent men and women.

Let me give you some words of wisdom, because you don't want to abandon your Dynamic Rational Selfishness Weapon when you desperately need it. And desperation could make you do just that. I guarantee that continuous economic hardship brings out the worst in many people. Jealousy, envy, anger, hate, revenge, covetousness and despair will be plentiful. The misery index soars to the stratosphere. You certainly don't want to discover that you've become a card-carrying member of the irrational selfishness club.

When the "you know what" hits the fan, you might suddenly find yourself in despair. Economic catastrophe effects everyone, even those who properly prepared for it. You begin seeking short-term band-aids to stop the monetary bleeding to the exclusion of long-term solutions. I understand you might have to resort to some immediate solutions ASAP. However the short-term mentality completely takes over your life. The next thing you know, you're running with a pack of irrationally selfish people. You forget that you exist as a Rationally Selfish Individual. You trade in your Dynamic Weapons for a pittance. You're happy just to survive another day. You forget that the impeccable warrior not only tunes himself to survive, he (she) thrives. He understands reality and he uses his knowledge to succeed in his endeavors. The warrior obtains peace of mind because he is confident in his ability to overcome challenges and obstacles. He believes that he will achieve his goals and desires.

As a Rationally Selfish Individual you must begin eliminating your despair by discovering long-term solutions to your woes. Any short-term solutions you adopt must not contradict your game plan. I know. That's easier said than done. Nobody's perfect. Just do the best you can, because tomorrow becomes today rather quickly. Thinking logically and rationally about the future keeps you grounded. You don't want to allow feelings of hopeless to cause your negative emotions to run rampant. That's what irrationally selfish people do. The impeccable warrior controls his thoughts, feelings and actions.

If you remain in the company of irrationally selfish people your misery level will likely shoot sky high up into the lower reaches of space. I guess you realize that negative emotions and misery go hand in hand, joining in an unholy matrimony in the ether. By the way, the ether I'm talking about has nothing to do with the heavens. It's a place of mindless, where the senses have been put to sleep by a Social Altruist's anesthesia. If you allow this to happen to you, you can kiss bye bye anything based on values or merit. Fortunately, I have confidence in your ability to exist as a Rationally Selfish Individual—and I know you will use your Dynamic Weapons to conquer life's illusions. That's what the impeccable warrior does.

Conclusion

The Rationally Selfish Individual develops his ability to adapt to change. He realizes that those who anticipate future change profit from their foresight. It's reaction and adaptation, not comfort zones that moves people forward. It's nice to feel comfortable, but don't allow your comfort zone to enslave you to a life of quiet desperation. Joyfully look forward to a future that offers you happiness and success.

If you desire a life of the Rational Selfishness, you must TAKE CHARGE of your thoughts, feelings and emotions. You act as a Rationally Selfish Individual acts. You achieve fulfillment in many areas of your life. You become an impeccable warrior. Happily, you possess the Dynamic Weapons to do just that. Yes! You are on your way.

The Rationally Selfish Individual exercises immense power as an impeccable warrior who wields Dynamic Weapons. As he moves closer to becoming a Master of Life, he begins generating massive amounts of positive energy which makes it more likely that he will attract whatever he needs to accomplish his goals and desires.

CHAPTER SIX

YOUR DYNAMIC WEAPONS – A DAILY AFFAIR

Life is a collection of all your moments. You have the choice on how you want to live your life, and your existence adds up to the sum of your days. How do you feel about your time on earth so far? Do you actively plan your day or do you just let it happen. The Rationally Selfish Individual plans his day, while the irrationally selfish person just whittles his time away, often in mindless, self-defeating activities.

Morning Time

How do you feel when you wake up in the morning? Your thoughts upon awakening can make or break your day. Do you think "Oh my God, it's another day" or do you silently say "Thank you God for another day." You might express your gratitude or dismay with different phrases than the ones I supplied. I'm sure you get the idea. Your first thoughts in the morning can set the tone for how you feel throughout the day. In the next chapter, I supply you with a Dynamic Weapon and some powerful ammo that will help you start your day off on the right track.

Even though the morning can seem harsh and somehow arrives earlier than we wish, we must start it off on the right track. You've heard about getting up on the wrong side of the bed. Too many mornings like that results in our hopes and dreams becoming hopelessly misplaced. I doubt if you'll find them at the lost and found.

I don't have to tell you how the irrationally selfish individual starts his day. His morning could include hangovers, undesirable thoughts, negative emotions and a general sluggishness that makes an endless sleep seem like a blessing. When he or she stumbles through the day with a negative attitude and a grouchy disposition, unfortunately crossing your path, you will need to put your Anti-Irrational Selfishness Weapon into action. Ready, Aim, Fire.

You should know by now that the Rationally Selfish Individual goes against the grain and the flow of traffic from time to time. You don't want to open your eyes and in the process close them by waking up as Mr. Mrs. or Ms. Average Joe (Jo). You go to bed as a Rationally Selfish Individual and you wake up as one. You possess the Dynamic Weapon and you exist as the Dynamic Weapon of Rational Selfishness.

When you wake up you should envision your goals and objectives. It's nice if you include some pleasurable activities. The impeccable warrior embraces the pleasures of the body, mind and spirit. Of course, his pleasures enhance his being. If you look at your obstacles as challenges that you conquer, you stand a good chance at filling your day with joy. If you also possess a strong sense of humor, your life offers you rewards that the irrationally selfish person will never experience, even when he takes a long anticipated vacation.

Time for words of caution. It's impossible to successfully bury your thoughts, feeling and emotions. You must deal with them—or else they will surface at the worst possible moment. The comic strip character Pogo said *"We have met the enemy and he is us."* I know. It's bad enough having to deal with Social Altruists and irrationally selfish people. On top of that you have to deal with yourself. Guess what? You are in luck. As mentioned, in the next chapter you discover a new Dynamic Weapon that holds some mighty powerful ammo. Yes, you will smoke out the nasty BS that sabotages you. You get the thrill of hunting some ornery self-sabotaging critters. Ready, Aim, Fire.

The impeccable warrior TAKES CHARGE of his thoughts, feelings and actions. As a Rationally Selfish Individual, you are the one in control. You choose your destiny. You arm yourself with Dynamic Weapons.

Let's say you need more information in order to handle a delicate situation. It's wise to seek the knowledge of people who not only believe in the supremacy of reason, but who also developed their intuitive powers. Hey, I just described the Rationally Selfish Individual. According to Robert Ringer you should *"Ignore all irrational remarks and actions of normal people and all remarks and actions — irrational or otherwise — of neurotic people."* It's prudent to disregard anything irrationally selfish people tell you, although it's possible that these reality evaders might supply something of value every once in a while. Anyway, why would you seek the advice of people who adopt irrationality as a predominant lifestyle. Once the evidence is in, you step back, analyze it and use your Dynamic Mind Power Weapon to arrive at at a correct conclusion.

William Ernest Henley wrote the poem "Invictus", which ended with the profound lines: *"I am the master of my fate, I am the captain of my soul."* And indeed you are.

Your Definite Purpose in Life

As mentioned, your morning sets the course for the rest of the day. Do you feel a burst of energy when you wake up? Maybe, maybe not. I admit that some mornings I wobble out of bed wondering if Mr. Sandman stole my energy as I drifted off to sleep. How do I retrieve it? In the next chapter, you will discover a Dynamic Weapon that increases your mental and emotional energy. Discovering it was one of the most rewarding experiences of my life. Fortunately, there's something else that will pump up your energy every day of your life. It's Definiteness of Purpose. You must possess a DEFINITE PURPOSE in Life. When used with your Dynamic Weapons of Rational Selfishness and Mind Power it converts into extra potent ammo that destroys failure, frustration and misery. You'll have Social Altruists and irrationally selfish people on the run. Here's what Napoleon Hill has to say about it.

"Definiteness of purpose is the starting point of all achievement. Don't be like a ship without a rudder, powerless and directionless. Decide what you want, find out how to get it, and then take daily action toward achieving your goal. You will get exactly only what you ask and work for."

Make up your mind today what it is you want and then start today to go after it! Do it now! Successful people move on their own initiative, but they know where they are going before they start."

That's what the Rationally Selfish Individual does. When faced with impending purposelessness, uncertainty or procrastination, he supplies his Dynamic Rational Selfishness Weapon with the ammo of DEFINITE PURPOSE. He understands that an existence without purpose stands out as one of life's illusions. He conquers it with deadly precision.

Important recommendation: Read Napoleon Hill's 'Think and Grow Rich" and "The Law of Success." In fact, I'm going to re-read these masterpieces.

When you look at today's important activities, how do you feel about them? Are they challenges that you happily look forward to conquering —or do you see them as burdens that weigh you down? You can see why possessing a DEFINITE PURPOSE makes life worthwhile. People without a purpose actually hold on to one "purpose." Getting the work day or work week over with so they can indulge in some mindless activities. Now I'm not saying that you shouldn't relax and enjoy some pleasurable activities, but if that's your purpose in life, you have a real problem. After a productive day of working on my DEFINITE PURPOSE, I love to slowly sip some Chardonnay or Brandy and listen to my favorite music. The Rationally Selfish Individual enjoys the pleasures of the body, mind and spirit purposefully.

Your DEFINITE PURPOSE must inspire you. Without inspiration, you won't stick to it. Don't just decide on something willy-nilly. The Rationally Selfish Individual knows what his (her) DEFINITE PURPOSE is because he lives by his highest values.

Once you decide on your DEFINITE PURPOSE, a deadly enemy will confront you. Even though it's one of the best friends of the irrationally selfish individual, it will attempt to befriend you. It goes by the name of Procrastination. It tempts you with the illusion of mindless short-term pleasures. Like they say, with this kind of friend who needs enemies. As soon as it arrives on the scene you pull out your Dynamic Weapons of Mind Power and Rational Selfishness. Hopefully, you're not sitting around naked and unprepared. Never forget that you are in charge of the unique and powerful experience that manifests as your life.

Once it's time to work, get going. Procrastination might have you lamenting about what you should do, causing you to shuffle papers or check out social media fluff. You need to make a list of your "A" activities. I have mine on a Word doc. with the simple title of "Action." Just start on one of those activities. Albert Einstein stated *"Nothing happens until something moves."* You need to take action, then more action. The Rationally Selfish Individual packs his Dynamic Weapons with plenty of action.

Let's face it. You will face many challenges that seemingly come out of nowhere. That is what makes life, well life. Often events appear random and unpredictable. Existence isn't some lily white phenomenon

8 Dynamic Weapons for Conquering Life's Illusions

that you can statistically inventory, predict and perfectly forecast. In fact, it appears quite chaotic. The Rationally Selfish Individual finds order in chaos. Sometimes unpleasant events happen to you and the people around you. How you act and what you do during times of trials and tribulations define you. Once again we turn to Norman Vincent Peale. *"Become a possibilitarian. No matter how dark things seem to be or actually are, raise your sights and see possibilities - always see them for they're always there."* What great advice! Brian Tracy says *"I believe through learning and application of what you learn, you can solve any problem, overcome any obstacle and achieve any goal that you can set for yourself."* You are learning how to us your Dynamic Weapons. The Rationally Selfish Individual overcomes obstacles and achieves his goals by conquering life's illusions.

I think you agree that it's worth your while to meet life's events with high energy, especially since there will be times when that prankster Murphy from Murphy's Law shows up to spoil your day. His motto is *"Anything that can go wrong, will go wrong."* Success in life is positively correlated with the amount of times you failed and were able to rebound by pursuing newer and better opportunities. Do you you know that successful people failed many times before they discovered the road to success? You don't think I discovered the virtue of Rational Selfishness overnight. I can tell you many tales of failure, frustration and heartbreak.

You need to accept failure as a cost of learning and more than that; a measure of learning as well. One of my goals in supplying you Dynamic Weapons is my desire to help you avoid the mistakes I made. Yes! You can conquer life's illusions much quicker than I conquered them. Once upon a time, I believed I dressed as the Emperor of Rational Selfishness. Reality exposed me as the emperor with no clothes. In my defense, I was unaware of 4 important Dynamic Weapons. Fortunately, that was then and this now.

If you want excel at your DEFINITE PURPOSE or any other activity, you need to be proactive. You've heard that practice makes perfect. You reach mastery by gaining as much experience as possible. You work as hard and as effectively as you can; then one day you arrive at the place you always dreamed about. Don't permit anyone to discourage you with the nonsense that you must discover some magical formula of realization or spend years learning the 5823 rules of success. Once again we turn to Robert Ringer for some important advice. *"Don't allow yourself to be intimidated by know-it-alls who thrive on bestowing their knowledge on insecure people. Mentally close your ears and put blinders on your eyes, and move relentlessly forward with the knowledge that what someone else knows is not relevant. In the final analysis, what is relevant to your success is what you know and what you do."*

Social Altruists and irrationally selfish people often masquerade as know-it-alls. They secretly want to see you to fail miserably. Your success and happiness threatens their shaky anti-life foundations. Your Dynamic Weapons remain your best defense against these people. You can see why I introduced you to the Dynamic Mind Power Weapon. You possess a weapon that easily disposes of mental midgets.

You decide on your DEFINITE PURPOSE in Life which should supply you a positive attitude and the motivation to get moving. Next you take immediate action to gain the raw experience you need.

As we discussed earlier there are two prime ways to gain insight: through wisdom or through woe. When you can't gain the proper advice or pre-learned insight that means you're going to have to figure it out on your own. You're faced with the slow trial and error method. My fervent desire is to eliminate much of the woe you will experience by winging it. I am supplying you Dynamic Weapons so you can conquer life's illusions. In addition, I'm quoting other people who can help you. You can't afford to live your life in despair. Instead of running away from problems you conquer them. Most of the time things never are as bad as you think they are. It's much better to directly face your challenges than to cowardly run away from them. The Rationally Selfish Individual TAKES CHARGE of his thoughts, feelings and actions. He reigns as an impeccable warrior who uses his Dynamic Weapons to conquer his enemies, even the ones that have invaded his body, mind and spirit. Do you have a history of conquering the challenges that life throws your way? If not, you can start making history. Are you an impeccable warrior who soars with confidence? Do you possess the motivation and enthusiasm to action?

8 Dynamic Weapons for Conquering Life's Illusions

Here's a list of important questions for you to answer.

1. Have you decided on your DEFINITE PURPOSE in Life?
2. Have you written your long term goals, intermediate goals and short term goals down or typed them in a Word doc?
3. Are your most urgent desires being met?
4. Are things going according to your plans, and if they aren't, are you adjusting your plans accordingly?
5. Do you allow your desires, plans and goals to fire up your enthusiasm? If you're not fired up, you need to rethink your DEFINITE PURPOSE.
6. Are you taking purposeful actions to accomplish your goals and desires?
7. When making plans that will propel you towards your DEFINITE PURPOSE or any secondary goals, are you big picture oriented, detail oriented or both? It's best to see the big picture and the details clearly.
8. Do you have the amount of time and resources necessary to complete your goals? Often you have to make time and discover the necessary resources. Your DEFINITE PURPOSE deserves everything you can give it.
9. Do you anticipate the pleasurable activities you will indulge after a productive day of working on your DEFINITE PURPOSE and secondary goals?
10. Do you give yourself a reward for completing goals? Pleasurable rewards can spur you on to greater achievement. Enjoy life. After all, you're not a cold emotionless drone. If you feel a nothingness while working on your DEFINITE PURPOSE you need to step back ask yourself why you are not enjoying the journey. Working on your goals should supply you pleasure and satisfaction.
11. Are you ready to effectively use your psychological arsenal of Dynamic Weapons to conquer life's illusions?

The Rationally Selfish Individual experiences the joy of his existence. He (she) TAKES CHARGE of his thoughts, feelings and actions, generating positive energy and attracting the things and circumstances he needs to succeed in his endeavors. His life expands as a wondrous adventure. He experiences pleasure and ecstasy regardless of whether other members of the economic system are experiencing good times or suffering bad times.

Isn't this exciting! You, the Rationally Selfish Individual exercises immense power as an impeccable warrior who wields Dynamic Weapons. As you move closer to becoming a Master of Life you will begin to generate massive amounts of positive energy which makes it more likely that you will attract whatever you need to accomplish your goals and desires. You will easily succeed at anything you put your mind to because you possess the Dynamic Mind Power Weapon.

A Recipe for Personal Misery

As we talked about earlier, your morning usually defines your day. Do you feel overwhelmed or are you ready to rise to the challenge? A person who has allowed irrational selfishness to take control of his life might go to pieces over little things like getting dressed or making the bed. A severely depressed person won't even be able to attend to his basic needs. You can allow difficulties and responsibilities to drag you down as insurmountable problems or you can decide to transform them into challenges that you conquer with your Dynamic Weapons. You make the choice.

Let's consider the unfortunate person who wakes up in the morning overwhelmed with negativity. Do you think he (she) has an easy time getting out of bed. Can you imagine how difficult it is for him to find the motivation to take any productive action? He generates so much negative energy, that even if he manages to pull himself out of bed, he attracts negative people and circumstances, depleting the minuscule amount of positive energy he did possess. By time nightfall arrives, he feels extremely tired, suffering from the despair of his daily whipping. His only solace is sleep, that is if the curse of insomnia doesn't cause sleeplessness.

Obviously, we just described a person who never discovered the Dynamic Weapon of Rational Selfishness. He lives his miserable life as an irrationally selfish person who allowed Social Altruists to pollute his body, mind and spirit with the anti-life philosophy of selflessness and self-sacrifice. We see an unfortunate soul who doesn't know he possesses every right to live for his own sake. How could we even think about him feeling motivated enough to take positive actions to accomplish anything worthwhile when he's smothered by life's illusions. He will never see problems as challenges that could strengthen him once he acted effectively to solve them.

The Rationally Selfish Individual understands things don't always go as planned. He realizes that he must continually make adjustments in order to accomplish his goals and desires. That's why he prefers seeing problems as challenges. If the time arrives where he suddenly feels overwhelmed, he will back off, replenish his positive energy and rediscover his bearings. Let's consider the saying "When the going gets tough, the tough get going." This is good advice unless more action sends you spiraling further and further away from accomplishing your DEFINITE PURPOSE or any other goals and desires you're working on. You could be well past the point of diminishing returns. Harry Browne makes it clear in his marvelous book on sales "Secret of Selling Anything." He says that another all-time sales fallacy is the statement *"When the going gets tough, the tough get going. When the going gets tough, I usually take a vacation."* As Kenny Rogers sings *"You got to know when to hold'em, know when to fold'em."* The Rationally Selfish Individual knows that sometimes it best to retreat and restock his Dynamic Weapons for renewed action.

The irrationally selfish person will take anything bad that befalls him as an personal attack. He laments that this shouldn't have happened to him, that once again he's a victim of a grave injustice. Sure, injustice runs rampant in a world created by Social Altruists and their benefactors, members of the parasitical elite. However, the more he focuses on injustice instead of self-responsibility the more he loses his grip on reality and allows fear to take over his sense of life. Fear lurks behind all of the negative emotions. When Social Altruists arrive on the scene to "help" him, he doesn't possess the necessary Dynamic Weapons to repel them.

When an overwhelmingly negative attitude shapes your reality, you attract more negativity in the form of negative people. Like attracts like. It only gets worse when a group of irrationally selfish people throw a pity party. If you happen to find yourself at one their gatherings I hope you're walking proud as a Dynamic Rational Selfishness Weapon with your Dynamic Anti-Irrational Selfishness Weapon at your side.

Let's explore a harrowing nightmare. You find yourself at a pity party surrounded by hundreds of irrationally selfish men and women. Suddenly, you realize you're sitting naked at a bar crying in your beer over all the sad tales of misery and despair you somehow couldn't resist. Someone sits by you slurring something about how undeserved it all is. He or she finally becomes angry and in a high screechy voice claims there ought to be a law, the government ought to do something. You can't tell if it's a man or a woman going on and on about social injustice. You make an effort to escape your predicament. You get up, turn around and discover a frightening situation. You're confronted by a Social Altruist who smiles at you, slaps you on the back and gives you that knowing wink of an eye. In your drunken state of mindless you vaguely remember possessing some kind of weapon, but it's nowhere to be found. You realize you are trapped. There is no escape. You let out a terrible scream, hoping it will awaken you from your horrible nightmare. You wake up with the determination to never again indulge in irrational selfishness. You make a lifetime pledge to always live as a Rationally Selfish Individual, even in your dreams. You promise to keep your psychological arsenal of Dynamic Weapons clean and ready for action at all times.

It's not always possible to avoid negative people. Still, it's not in your best interest to interact and socialize with negative people when it's possible for you to ignore them. You must realize they allow their reality to be shaped by other negative people. You have the perverse spectacle of irrationally selfish people feeding on each other. Eventually Social Altruists get in on the "feast" and consume what's left of their minds and souls. Can you imagine the emptiness of the irrationally selfish person. His only "weapons" are denial, projection and transference. His basic personality traits along with his unhappy situations decide which impotent weapon he will favor. He also has the option of indulging in mind-numbing activities in order to alleviate his suffering. Life's illusions have him sewed up in a Social Altruist's bag of tricks. Fortunately, you possess the Dynamic Weapons to conquer life's illusions.

Let's say you inadvertently or carelessly allow negative people in your life. You're amazed to see them multiplying like rabbits. The next thing you know you are witnessing a sick competition where first prize goes to the person who displays the most irrationally selfish traits. Much to your surprise, your reason, logic and rationality wins you the "booby" prize. Since you're such a "terrible" individual you think that maybe you'll be kicked out of the "league of irrationality." No such luck. Even irrationally selfish people have watched enough sporting events to know there has to be a winner and a loser. In your state of shock you temporarily forget about your Dynamic Weapons. Suddenly, you feel some evil force draining your vital energy. Much to your dismay you realize that energy vampires are sucking you dry. Just in time you remember you possess your Dynamic Anti-Irrational Selfishness Weapon. You have just enough energy left to Ready, Aim, Fire. You let out a sigh of relief at your close call.

Anger, Energy, Rational Selfishness and You

A day filled with negative energy taxes a person mentally and emotionally. Eventually, the negative individual finds solace in drugs, alcohol or sleep, that is if sleep is possible. Circumstances can beat down a Rationally Selfish Individual, but he owns the Dynamic Weapons that allow him to fight back and eventually rise up to victory. The irrationally selfish person permits adverse conditions to keep him in an unhappy state of despair and defeat. His only hope for salvation rides on the possibility of Social Altruists coming to the "rescue."

Depending on a Social Altruist for your salvation is like members of a hen house depending on the fox for their salvation. Now that I think of it, I guess we can call Social Altruists humanitarians. What is a Vegetarian? Someone who lives on a diet of grains, pulses, nuts, seeds, vegetables and fruits with, or without, the use of dairy products and eggs. What is a humanitarian? Someone who lives on a diet which consists of the body, mind and spirit of humans. In other words he symbolically eats humans. That's a good description of a Social Altruist.

When Social Altruists and irrationally selfish people join together the quality of living begins to go down for everyone. It's difficult to imagine the negative impact their anti-life philosophy of selflessness and self-sacrifice has on the innocent. Once they enlist the help of the government's apparatus of violent compulsion and coercion to make people fall in line, the social consequences rack up a disturbing amount of innocent victims. It's time to get out your Dynamic Weapons. You know which ones you need. Ready, Aim, Fire. Ready, Aim, Fire. Ready, Aim, Fire, Fire Fire, Fire, Reload, Ready, Aim, Fire, Fire, Fire, Fire, Fire, Reload---------------------------------.

We demonstrated that drug laws and drug prohibition negatively affect the economy and the population—giving the USA the most incarcerated population in any part of the world. You own your life, therefore you own your body. You have the natural right to consume anything you want. Yes, you possess the right to indulge in irrationally selfish behavior. However, actions have consequences. You remain responsible for your actions. If you get drunk or drugged up, causing damage to someone's person or property, you must pay the piper. The Rationally Selfish Individual TAKES CHARGE of his thoughts, feelings and actions.

You adopt Rational Selfishness as a way of life. You do everything possible to take control of your body, mind and spirit. You make sure you carry your Dynamic Weapons at all times. Much to your chagrin you notice it's virtually impossible to completely avoid Social Altruists and irrationally selfish people unless you decide to hole up somewhere as a hermit. Maybe you work with some of them or have relatives who indulge in irrationality daily. It's possible to run into a head case at the grocery store. Eventually someone pushes your button. In the heat of the moment you forget you exist as a Rationally Selfish Individual. You lose your head and become angry. Your anger leads to an explosive outburst that destabilizes you. You're no longer the impeccable warrior.

I admit the above has happened to me. I temporarily abandoned my Dynamic Weapons and stupidly slipped back into irrational selfishness. Fortunately, I'm past extreme anger. I can still feel incensed, but I take control of my momentary feelings and refuse to act on them. It's rather unpleasant to feel washed out because you allowed your positive energy to dissipate in a frenzy of negative emotions.

When you allow anger to cause you to lose control, you end up saying some pretty bad things, possibly burning bridges that you wish you had not burned. The irrationally selfish person can receive a quick rush from his anger, but it's only temporary. The Rationally Selfish Person possesses so much positive energy that he will immediately feel drained from his outburst. You must understand that anger will not supply you any pleasure. It's in your best interest to have your Dynamic Weapons ready at all times. You can see the importance as living as the Dynamic Rational Selfishness Weapon. Your Dynamic Mind Power Weapon will help you deal with anger. In Chapter Seven, I supply you another Dynamic Weapon that will empower you.

Anger masquerades as a siren or temptress that leads you down the dark path of despair and defeat. The temptation lies in the unfortunate fact that lashing out at people can be addictive because of the brain chemistry that is activated and changed in fits of rage. The addiction is an illusion. In reality, anger manifests as a vampire who sucks out all your positive energy. The irrationally selfish person lives in a world of illusion. Fortunately, this is not you. You live as an impeccable warrior who uses his Dynamic Weapons to conquer life's illusions.

What goes out comes back in. When you infest your life and lives of others with anger it boomerangs, coming back to inflict irreparable harm on your body, mind and spirit. On top of that it will shatter relationships that are dear to you. It's detrimental to your long-term survival. Irrational selfishness knows no bounds. Anyone who easily falls to the temptation of anger will even direct it towards those who can offer him value for value relationships. Talk about self-sabotage. The Rationally Selfish Individual cherishes value for value relationship. He's adverse to ignorantly terminating precious friendships and intimacies.

Let's explore the effects of relying on the negative emotions in your daily affairs. I making sure that you never abandon your Dynamic Weapons as I foolishly did on several occasions. What you don't learn through wisdom your learn through woe. Never forget that wisdom will always be one of the impeccable warrior's best friends. He continually supplies his Dynamic Weapons with this powerful ammo.

Living in anger, despair and hate is especially taxing and exhausting on your physical body. It could cause you to eat too much or not enough, drink yourself to oblivion and abuse dangerous drugs. The Rationally Selfish Individual doesn't throw the baby out with bath water. He knows that food, alcohol and drugs can offer a person therapeutic effects. Unfortunately, the irrationally selfish person fails to recognize the law of diminishing returns. He goes well beyond whats good for him. He descends into an abyss of abusive behavior, destroying himself and those around him.

As a Rationally Selfish Individual you want to look and feel healthy, confident and energetic. Negative thoughts and self-defeating behavior has a tendency to cause premature aging—plaguing you with some serious health problems. The effects on your body will be visible for all to see. People will first notice the unfortunate results on your face. Wrinkles and lines will begin to form where they didn't exist before. Sadly, you will begin looking much older than your age. I'm sure this unhappy fact bothers the ladies more than it does the men, although nobody wants to look like he's "over the hill." In addition, you become mentally exhausted from continuous expressions of irrationally selfish behavior. If you are constantly worried and consumed by anger, you will burnout very quickly. Your ability to work on your DEFINITE PURPOSE will be seriously compromised—that is if you still remember it. Should negative emotions and irrational selfishness suddenly threaten you it's time to reach for your Dynamic Weapons. You know what you need. In case you're still uncertain which ones to pull out in this situation, I will spell it out for you. You put your Dynamic Weapons of Rational Selfishness, Anti-Irrational Selfishness and Mind Power into action.

You want to achieve the results you desire. The positive energy you dissipate when you give into negative emotions could be better applied to your personal and professional life. Rationally Selfish Individuals do not want to hang around negative people. It's difficult to build value for value relationships when you only attract irrationally selfish people into your life.

How about the effect negative emotions and irrationally selfish behavior has on your spirit. It's bad enough to cause great damage to your body and mind, but vandalizing your spirit wrecks something much deeper within you. When you find your spirit crushed your basic essence will be crushed as well. The irrationally selfish person fails to realize that the destruction of one's spirit amounts to the assassination of his personality and motivation. Emptiness causes a person to become alienated from himself, his society, his world and even the universe. He has no way to spiritually connect with existence. The walking dead lead a very lonely life. The more he (she) surrounds himself with other people in an effort to become part of humanity, the lonelier he becomes. Have you ever been to a party where people who wear magazine smiles drink, laugh, converse, cut up and act cheerful, but you know it's all an illusion. The atmosphere is so polluted, so oppressive that it almost suffocates you. You don"t feel clean until you leave the party, walk outside, look at the twinkling starlight, breathe fresh air and allow the vast universe to supply you a sense of freedom.

Most people are so scared of something negative happening and hearing the critique of their peers that they allow fear to beat them down. Fear is a powerful motivator. It provides you a useful service when it saves your life or your reputation. When it controls your life it brings you failure, frustration and misery. A person who has sold his "soul" to Social Altruists abandons any pretense at Rational Selfishness. His irrational selfishness guarantees fear takes charge of his life. The only way he can hold it at bay is by indulging in mind-numbing activities. Still, fear lurks in the background waiting to strike at a moment's notice. The Rationally Selfish Individual deals with irrational fear by resorting to his Dynamic Weapons. Sometimes it takes an impressive counter-attack to cause it to retreat. Because of the nature of existence, you will never completely eradicate fear. Happily you can greatly diminish the negative influence it has on your life.

The Rationally Selfish Individual takes action and places himself squarely in the game of life. How else will he accomplish his DEFINITE PURPOSE or anything else for that matter. You might say that he works to capture happiness and success. I'm letting you in on an important secret. The Rationally Selfish Individual, the impeccable warrior understands that the journey supplies him happiness, success and fulfillment. After all, the end result is part of the journey and the starting point of a new journey within the complete journey of life. I'm sure you realize happy memories supply you much pleasure. However, when you lament about the past you stir up guilt and other negative emotions. When you fear what may happen in the future you unleash the unpleasantness of anxiety. The Rationally Selfish Individual carefully plans for the future which allows him to experience the joy of his existence today.

Let's Rock the Boat

    Most people are too scared to "rock the boat" because of the threat of social embarrassment or even worse rejection. Fear and lack of self-confidence to handle the vicissitudes of life cause most people to dread change. It's so easy to remain in your comfort zone. I admit relaxing in one is rather nice, that is until it becomes your prison. Once you feel comfortable in a prison of your own making, you fail to see that your DEFINITE PURPOSE escaped long ago. You keep performing the same mundane duties day in and day out. Your mindless "pleasures" barely give you satisfaction. As the days whiz on by you wonder where it all went. You're oblivious to the fact that you possess the key that opens the door to your cell. It's possible that long ago you found the courage to escape. You unlocked your cell door, walked out, looked around and became disoriented and confused. In your dazed condition you turned around, walked back into your cell, re-locked the door and experienced a vague feeling of comfort knowing you were back home. Fortunately you have company. Your fellow inmates are irrationally selfish people. You work and play together "enjoying" mind numbing, soul shrinking activities. It's really quite a community run by the "benevolence" of Social Altruists. For your own good, they set down one iron law you must obey. The penalty for disobeying it is the death sentence. Your masters carry it out by stripping you of your irrational selfishness. The iron law that is punishable by death is "Don't rock the boat." Rumor has it that no one has ever been caught disobeying it.
    A person who captures Rational Selfishness as a lifestyle walks right out of his self-made prison. Do you wonder why the irrationally selfish inmates in the above story never received the "death penalty." It's been said that most people who are afraid to rock the boat, truth me told,

aren't anywhere close to capable enough to get the boat to notice them. In addition, the boat would knock down any fearful man or woman who happens to run into it. Grovelling on his knees doesn't exactly thrill the impeccable warrior. He knows that success is what you do *after* you are knocked down. He courageously gets back on his feet. I'm sure you realize that the impeccable warrior soars as a Rationally Selfish Individual and visa versa.

Your Dynamic Weapons empower you to excel as a Rationally Selfish Individual. Is there any reason why you can't effectively use them to conquer life's illusions? Can you see any reason why you shouldn't experience the joy of your existence every single day? I would certainly think not. I have some great news for you. You will hit the jackpot by seizing three more Dynamic Weapons.

Let's sum it up with a statement that ought to tickle your imagination. The impeccable warrior can rock the boat, allow the boat to rock him, become one with the boat, transcend the boat or realize the boat doesn't exist.

Rational Selfishness, Hangups and Illusions

Personal hangups interfere with your ability to enjoy the pleasures of the body, mind and spirit. When you conquer hangups, you conquer illusions because hangups are illusions. These dregs of personal development prevent you from experiencing the joy of your existence. You must realize that anything keeping you down is artificial, is born from illusion. Irrationally selfish people place blame for their predicament on anyone and anything except themselves. You take full responsibility for your decisions, choices and actions. How do you define an impeccable warrior, a Rationally Selfish Individual? He (she) is a person who TAKES CHARGE of his thoughts, feelings and actions. Maybe you're tired of hearing about it. You might think "How long is he going to keep harping on this. I get it, really I do." Well, until you internalize it, wield your Dynamic Weapons with deadly precision and live as a Rationally Selfish Individual you don't get it. Still, don't let it bother you. It took me a long time to get it. Occasionally I played with the fires of irrational selfishness and personal altruism. I finally got tired of suffering 3rd degree burns. It takes a long time to heal from the fires of foolishness.

The evil force of Social Altruism guarantees the re-occurrence of economic boom and bust cycles. Members of the political and financial establishment grabbed the anti-life philosophy of Social Altruism in order to plunder productive men and women. We thoroughly covered it in Chapter Four and supplied you with the Dynamic Unhampered Capitalism Weapon. As soon as someone starts feeding you the illusions of socialism, government interventionism or restrictions on voluntary exchanges you pull it out and blow their fallacies away. Associates of the anti-free enterprise clique base their faulty analysis on economic illusions. You'll never hear a logical argument from them, although you might unwillingly be "treated" to emotionalism, floating abstractions and propaganda. It's time to protect your personal liberty and economic freedom. Ready, Aim, Fire.

It's great to feel calm, cool and collected. The impeccable warrior feels that way. Nothing like thinking clearly, even when others are losing their heads over some significant or insignificant event. That's what you call control. You, the Rationally Selfish Individual increase your chances of success when you conquer negative emotions with your Dynamic Mind Power Weapon. You must use it with a calm, cool and collected attitude. Damn, you obviously have ice water circulating in your veins. On the other hand, your fire of passion and motivation melts away the enemies of your body, mind and spirit. That's some powerful ammo you possess. You're treating your Dynamic Weapons with "loving" care.

The impeccable warrior handles just about any situation thrown at him because he TAKES CHARGE of his thoughts, feelings and actions. You think maybe you've discovered an "open sesame" phrase. I've repeated it often enough. The important thing to remember is that you will never conquer life's illusions by indulging in irrationally selfish behavior. In addition, never fall for the illusions of Social Altruists. These perpetrators of human misery will eat your positive energy for breakfast. You wield and you are the Dynamic Rational Selfishness Weapon.

The Rationally Selfish Individual joyfully travels a path constructed of a series of productive and pleasurable days added together. It's not always easy, but with your Dynamic Weapons at your side you conquer the illusions that either slow you down or maliciously knock you off your chosen path. You resist the temptation to dabble in irrationally selfish behavior. Should you trip, stumble and fall into the arms of self-defeating behavior you know what to do. You immediately TAKE CHARGE of your thoughts, feeling and actions by saying "open sesame." Do you get it? You once again walk down the path of Rational Selfishness. Yes, you reign supreme as an impeccable warrior.

Words of wisdom. Practice makes the Master. You practice using your Dynamic Weapons until you master them. After that, you practice and practice more to remain a Master.

Do you ever wonder what the point of all of it is? Could it have something to do with the joy of everyday living? Let's go deeper and uncover the joy of your existence.

The Joy of Your Existence

What is our incredible journey of life all about? What's the point and the purpose of it all? I think we can assume a complex life goes well beyond reproduction. Humans don't have sex just to reproduce. Men and women express their basic essence in the pleasures of sex and intimacy. Mammals, Birds, Reptiles, and other types of animals display emotions, sense their environment around them, and express feelings and emotions. Unlike us, they can't contemplate their existence. You might dearly love your dog, but he will never tell you what it's all about. Still, when you watch your pets play you catch a glimpse of what the joy of existence is all about.

Here is the last section from an article I wrote called "The Lone Individual's Dark Night of the Soul."

The Morning After – The Hope of a New Day

"Oh God it's morning. I guess it was too much to ask for an endless sleep. I must force myself to rise. At least there's coffee. Hey, there is something in life that's worthwhile.

As I savor the first sip of my morning coffee, I glance out the front door. Maybe the sun will dispel the dark cloud that hangs over me—just as it has broken through the once threatening clouds to end a stormy morning.

The showers have left dreamy puddles in the street and on the sidewalks. My attention is suddenly diverted to a puddle on the sidewalk leading to my front porch. A robin has landed in it, chirping, joyously flapping its wings and splashing the water. It dawns on me that even a bird can express the pure joy of its existence.

I think of the lily of the valley. Does the lily of the valley know? To me all it does is soak up the sun or catch the falling raindrops, while a human worries about everything under the sun, dreading the darkening clouds that threaten his day.

Maybe if I could just experience the wonder and joy of my existence, forgetting the many days that brought me the pains, disappointments and sorrows that only humans can experience. I could move into the future—understanding that my past creations were illusions of limited consciousness. With my newly expanded awareness, I would create a world of love, serenity, joy and abundance. I would live my highest values—achieving happiness and peace of mind. I would live for now."

Maybe you've been through cloudy days and dark, rainy nights. It happens to us all. I knew about Rational Selfishness. I planned on practicing it religiously. Unfortunately, I was missing a few Dynamic Weapons. Foolishly, I allowed my most important one, Rational Selfishness, to run out of ammo. I fervently desire that it never happens to you. Fortunately, you receive the benefit of my years of experience. I am helping you remove the blocks and obstacles that tripped me up. You will discover the joy of your existence and retain it. Do you see a Dynamic Weapon in the making?

I'd like you to take a moment and think about the different aspects of life that give you a bundle of joy and happiness. What are some of your favorite things? How about the people who bring joy wherever they go? Let's go back to the year 1967 and the Summer of Love. The vocal group the Association sang a happy song called "Windy" written by Ruthann Friedman.

*"Who's peeking out from under a stairway
Calling a name that's lighter than air?
Who's bending down to give me a rainbow?
Everyone knows it's Windy.
Who's tripping down the streets of the city
Smiling at everybody she sees?
Who's reaching out to capture a moment?
Everyone knows it's Windy."*

I would say Windy expresses the joy of her existence.

Imagine you can find the possibility of bringing home joy even it is nowhere to be found. Maybe you think I'm crazy for even suggesting it, since your situation seems hopeless, although I doubt it. You know, I've supplied you enough Dynamic Weapons to move you hopefully and confidently on your way. I accept the fact that you could still be reeling from what appears to be hopeless trials and tribulations. Hang on, because the next Dynamic Weapon I supply you could activate the ones you acquired along the way. For now, just for the fun of it, entertain the possibility that you could fill your life with joy. I'm confident you'll eventually do just that.

The Choice is Yours

You can succumb to a chaotic world of illusion created by Social Altruists and irrationally people—or you can create the existence you desire by TAKING CHARGE of your thoughts, feelings and actions. The choice is yours. If you've read this far, I believe you already made a decision. You want to live your life as an impeccable warrior, a Rationally Selfish Individual. You need it as much as a drowning man needs air. You definitely don't want the last flicker of your life to go out in a cesspool of illogic, self-sacrifice and selflessness.

Many things happen in the world you have absolutely no control over. The Rationally Selfish Warrior firmly faces that fact. However, he knows he has close to 100% control of how he reacts to new information and stimulus. Sure, an unexpected event can throw him off guard and temporarily send him spinning down a dark hole. Happily, he learned to use his Dynamic Weapons effectively. His reaction time astonishes those who live in a haze of unreason and illusion. Just in time, he pulls out the appropriate Dynamic Weapon(s) and begins TAKING CHARGE of the situation. He might not win every battle, but he wins the war.

Robert Ringer reveals a marvelous theory in his outstanding best selling book "To Be or Not Be Intimidated" originally titled "Winning Through Intimidation." It applies to making money. He calls it the "Tortoise and Hare Theory." It's applicable to what we just discussed. *"The outcome of most situations in life are determined over the long term. The guy who gets off to a fast start merely wins a battle; the individual who's ahead at the end of the race wins the war. Battles are for ego-trippers; wars are for money-grippers."*

How do you increase your reaction time when dealing with unexpected events? Practice, practice and more practice. Although a situation might force you to shoot from the hip, it's still best to Ready, Aim, Fire. Your goal is to become more effective in the long run. That means you improve each and every day. Sure you will experience some days when you're stopped cold in your tracks, unmercifully bounced around or even slammed backwards. You might inadvertently stumble off the path and find yourself weaving back and forth towards some unwanted destination. What do you do in that case? You stop, reflect on your undesirable situation, come to a conclusion, TAKE CHARGE and begin marching back to your chosen path. It's possible you will determine the original path wasn't for you. It's critical that you make a correct decision when deciding on your DEFINITE PURPOSE.

Do you wonder what good luck or even bad luck has to do with it? To tell you the truth I'm not sure. I do know that when you develop the ability to control your thoughts, feelings and actions you increase your chances for good luck to bless you. Cause and effect relationships generally determine whether your results are good or bad. You're better off thinking in terms of the following formula. Correct decisions + purposive actions = desirable results. Yes it all adds up. You really do create your circumstances. You do it consciously or unconsciously. With your Dynamic Weapons, a level head and a positive attitude you can build the future you desire.

Conclusion

Experience teaches you that things don't always go as planned. It also lets you know that when you consistently and effectively work towards your DEFINITE PURPOSE and secondary goals you increase you chances of success. With a consistent effort day in and day out you set a up a reliable system of success. I must warn you that no matter how efficient you become, an unknown illusion can appear out of nowhere, viciously attacking your plans and desires. In the next chapter I supply you with a Dynamic Weapon that helps you recognize and conquer the illusion when it appears.

Your life is a series of thoughts, feelings and actions that make up your behavior. You achieve mastery by carefully and mindfully taking control of them. With accelerated awareness, you easily use the appropriate Dynamic Weapon(s) to diminish the effect negative emotions have on your body, mind and spirit.

CHAPTER SEVEN

DYNAMIC ACCELERATED AWARENESS WEAPON

You possess 5 Dynamic Weapons. In addition you exist as one of them, the Dynamic Rational Selfishness Weapon. It's time for you to capture another Dynamic Weapon.

Cults, cliques and organizations often obscure the steps to attaining accelerated awareness. They present some esoteric program you must follow day after day, month after month, year after year. In order to keep you interested, the guru or leader feeds you one morsel at a time. In addition you must completely surrender your current lifestyle for one that severely restricts your personal liberty and economic freedom.

You must realize that many people at the top view the world as a zero sum game. Your loss becomes their gain. As you slowly "progress" your power actually diminishes while the guru's power greatly increases. Can you imagine what a flock of "sheeple" does for the guru's already inflated ego. You can see why members of a cult appear as mindless idiots. What do you have left after you surrender your body, mind and spirit? A big zero. You already know that the impeccable warrior, the Rationally Selfish Individual takes control of his body, mind and spirit. Before he would allow a phony motivational or spiritual leader to swindle these out of him, he would have already put his Dynamic Weapons in action.

Obviously not all motivational and spiritual leaders are frauds. I already mentioned some great warriors and sages who can help you considerably. The real leader does not desire the status of a guru. He wants you to discover your own ability to become a leader.

The idea that only a chosen few can obtain a state of accelerated awareness is hopelessly outdated. Incidentally you've probably heard of higher awareness. I've used the term before. The problem I have with the term is that it makes it sound like awareness resides somewhere in the ether or the heavens. You know, something only New Age space cadets pursue. I don't have anything against the New Age movement,

Some of the Eastern Philosophy and Biblical Principles it's based on has passed the test of time. I just want you understand where were going and how we're getting there. Your Dynamic Weapons can be mental, emotional, physical and spiritual. However, you must understand they effectively use powerful ammunition made of logic, reason and intuition with deadly precision. You wield them to conquer life's illusions.

It appears members of the political and financial establishment rule us with an iron hand. Yes, they do possess considerable power. It amazes me the voters continue to elect "slave-masters." Social Altruists keep them in line with the "good of society" BS. On top of that these purveyors of human angst and degradation dish out the selflessness, self-sacrifice nonsense to the masses. No wonder so many people indulge in irrational selfishness to escape their misery. Fortunately, we know better. We stand tall as Rationally Selfish Individuals. As impeccable warriors we arm ourselves with Dynamic Weapons. When confronted with the enemies of personal liberty and economic freedom we Ready, Aim, Fire—as many times as necessary.

A New Dynamic Weapon

You've gained some mastery over your Dynamic Weapons. You're confident your Dynamic Rational Selfishness Weapon supplies you incredible personal power. As an impeccable warrior you live by the phrase "I TAKE CHARGE of my thoughts, feelings and actions." You repeat it when necessary. You take effective actions to achieve your goals. You continue to conquer life's illusions with your Dynamic Weapons. Yet, you don't appear to be closing in on what it is you so much desire. You feel frustrated and at your wit's end. You wonder how you are going to survive the challenges and obstacles life keeps throwing in your path. It's gotten so bad that dealing with Social Altruists and irrationally selfish people day in and day out wears you out. Incredibly, you even consider giving into irrationally selfish behaviors. If things aren't going to get any better, you might as well drink, smoke, drug it up or whatever else supplies you with immediate satisfaction.

I have to empathize with you. I certainly understand the appeal of irrationally selfish behavior. At times, I have allowed myself to partake of the serpent's apple. Sometimes I went the whole route and added a touch of unwise personal altruism to the equation. I don't think I have to go into the gory details about the results I achieved from this type of behavior. All I can say is that I paid a heavy price for my unfortunate actions. The piper always demands payment. Fortunately, out of my despair I discovered a gift of inestimable value. I captured the Dynamic Accelerated Awareness Weapon.

Your New Dynamic Weapon Helps You Conquer Your Own Irrational Selfishness

Whatever you do don't fall into the irrational selfishness trap like I fell into it. I was missing too many Dynamic Weapons including the Accelerated Awareness one. Once I acquired it and used it along with my Dynamic Anti-Irrational Selfishness Weapon, self-defeating behavior lost its ability to tempt me—at least a high percentage of the time. When you act with awareness you just can't consciously do things that aren't in your best interest. Sure, you might make a mistake now and then, but your new Dynamic Weapon guarantees you quickly change course.

Now I can't guarantee that you won't ever indulge in irrational selfishness. Fortunately, with your Dynamic Accelerated Awareness Weapon you will reverse course before you cause great harm to your body, mind and spirit. Along with your other Dynamic Weapons, you control a powerful psychological arsenal of attack and self-defense. Sure, we're all human. Nobody's perfect. We occasionally mess up. The Rationally Selfish Individual cuts down on the amount of times he messes up and he's quick to clean his messes up. What happens if you're on the verge of losing your cool? You stop, breathe in slowly and count from 10 to 0. During this time your remember you're an impeccable warrior who TAKES CHARGE of his thoughts, feelings and actions. You exist as the Dynamic Rational Selfishness Weapon who effectively uses his Dynamic Weapons with deadly precision. Life's illusions don't stand much of a chance against you.

Robert Meyer

A Series of Thoughts, Feelings and Actions

Your life is a series of thoughts, feelings and actions that make up your behavior. You achieve mastery by carefully and mindfully taking control of them. With accelerated awareness, you easily use the appropriate Dynamic Weapon(s) to diminish the effect negative emotions have on your body, mind and spirit. I was tempted to say you will eradicate them, but your emotions are a basic part of your being. You replace negative thoughts and feelings with their opposite. You have your Dynamic Mind Power Weapon. Along with your Dynamic Accelerated Awareness Weapon you will blast away the dregs of the mind and substitute them with empowering thoughts and feelings. Shortly, you will discover some incredibly, powerful ammo for the above 2 Dynamic Weapons. The challenge is whether or not you choose to use it.

Rational Selfishness is an everyday occurrence. You can't succumb to irrational selfishness one day, embark on Social Altruism the next day then expect bounce back to Rational Selfishness the following day. It's impossible. The day arrives when you don't have enough energy to rebound back to the glory of an impeccable warrior. You don't build the habit of TAKING CHARGE of your thoughts, feelings and action by practicing them every third day. The bad habits you stupidly indulge in on the other two days overwhelm you, taking control of your floundering way of life.

Maybe you're still making mistakes that cause your thoughts and feelings to become confused. You don't know which way to turn. You understand that nothing happens until something moves but you have no direction. I've felt that way before. It finally occurred to me to search for my Dynamic Weapons. Gee, what did I do with them? Since you exist as the Dynamic Rational Selfishness Weapon, you find that one first. The others just suddenly turn up. Why? Because misplacing them is an illusion that you conquer as soon as your discover yourself. What happens if your state of mind is so bad you can't find yourself? Remember what Harry Browne said about taking a vacation. If it's necessary take one. He also said *"You have only one life, and no one else will live it for you. Shouldn't you take the time right now to figure out what that life is all about?"*

Important Recommendation: Read Harry Browne's "How I Found Freedom in an Unfree World." I've read it several times.

Look at the individuals who succeeded by satisfying the consumers' most urgent desires. Do you think their success happened overnight? Except for a few rare occasions, it took productive action day after day for him or her to accomplish his or her goals and desires. You can "bet your sweet bippy" that he or she possessed a DEFINITE PURPOSE in Life.

You might ask if these successful people used the Dynamic Weapons to succeed. Absolutely, although they might not be consciously aware of it. Some people have them firmly stored in the subconscious mind due to incredible childhood influences and positive genetic influences. I must tell you that I had to consciously seek them out. Until I reached the age of 28, I walked around blind, ignorant and naked—and didn't even know it. No matter where you are today, you can begin capturing the Dynamic Weapons. I believe that if I can do, you can do and much quicker than I did it.

Success Through Failure

You have a choice. Does failure make you smarter or do you allow it to permanently beat you down? You will make mistakes. There's no such thing as perfection in the sphere of human action. The most successful people in the world made plenty of mistakes. These courageous men and women kept plugging away, found out what didn't work and finally discovered the right formula for success. The Rationally Selfish Individual learns to turn failure into success. Tony Robbins, author of "Unlimited Power" and many other books on success, states *"I've come to believe that all my past failure and frustrations were actually laying the foundation for the understandings that have created the new level of living I now enjoy."* Understanding makes some mighty fine ammo for your Dynamic Weapons.

If you've completely missed the mark on your valiant attempts at success, think of the valuable lessons that failure provided you. Only a fool, an irrationally selfish fool would fail to learn from adversity. The Rationally Selfish Individual doesn't let failures flourish, then die in vain. He's grateful for the education he received. The irrationally selfish person ignores the lessons and instead plays the blame game. He's completely unaware that he's responsible for his life. If you begin feeling like your problems are solely caused by other people, it's time to get your Dynamic Weapons into immediate action.

When you think of each one of your failures, do see anything that could have helped you achieve better results? Did the lesson hit home? If not, you lack the Dynamic Accelerated Awareness Weapon—or maybe you possess it but don't know how to use it. I believe I introduced you to it, so you must lack the ability to properly use it effectively. I'm happy to say that I know where you can acquire some powerful ammo for your new Dynamic Weapon. Whether you go there or not is up to you.

The way you act when confronted with a difficult situation can make you or break you. You can TAKE CHARGE of your thoughts, feelings and actions, increasing your chances of cruising down the path of success—or you can give in to your negative emotions, allowing them to send you spiraling down the lone, dark road of failure and frustration. You know what the Rationally Selfish Individual, the impeccable warrior does. The irrationally selfish person usually falls apart by yielding to a pathetic emotional binge. He follows it up by indulging in some self-defeating behavior. If you find yourself feeling battered, bruised and bloody from a difficult battle, some opportunistic Social Altruists might get a whiff of your weakened state and come charging in for a dishonorable rescue. It's time to pull out your Dynamic Weapons of Rational Selfishness, Anti-Social Altruism and Anti-Irrational Selfishness. Just in case, make sure you have your other Dynamic Weapons available.

Let's say the beating you suffered causes you to lose sight of your DEFINITE PURPOSE in Life. To make matters worse, you doubt that you're really in charge of your thoughts, feelings and actions. You feel like such a failure. Believing you had control over anything must have been an illusion. Since misery loves company you seek out one of your irrationally selfish acquaintances for comfort. You commiserate about your debilitating failures over a Fifth of Jack Daniels. No matter what you come up with your "friend" can do one better. Pretty soon you're alternating between laughing and crying. In the background, you can hear Ray Charles singing "It's Crying Time Again." Once again the tears flow. The next thing you know you feel comforting arms embrace you. In your drunken state you think "I never realized it before, but he (she) is so sweet and understanding. You put on a weak smile. The last thing you hear before you completely pass out is the Beatles singing "He's a real Nowhere Man living in a nowhere land."

You wake up the next morning hungover, wondering where you are and what the hell happened. You realize you're naked. Rational Selfishness seems like a distant memory. The doorbell rings which doesn't help your aching head. You stumble over to the front door, look out the peep hole and ask who it is. A shady character says "I'm here to help you. Let me in." Oh my god! You realize it's a Social Altruist at the door and you're trapped in an irrationally selfish person's apartment. You think maybe if I close my eyes or just go unconscious it'll all go away.

I hope you never find yourself in that terrible predicament. Imagine abandoning your Dynamic Weapons and leaving home with an irrationally selfish individual. It's almost unthinkable.

We all desire love, affection and comfort. However you must realize that you won't receive anything genuine from Social Altruists and irrationally selfish people. You must TAKE CHARGE of your thoughts, feelings and actions. If you succumb to negative emotions you descend into an abyss of failure and frustration. In the marvelous book "The Law of Success" Napoleon Hill firmly states *"You have the power to control your thoughts and make them do your bidding."* That's what the Rationally Selfish Individual does.

Let's Take Charge

It's not enough to think you're in control of your thoughts, you must feel it through your whole being. Soon I will introduce you to some powerful ammo that will convince you that you're in charge of your thoughts, feelings and action.

Let's say you're still struggling to control your anger. I understand because it took me a long time to completely diminish it. Now I mainly express it in a controlled manner. You know, tough love or self-defense. For now, you need to try any trick in the book to catch yourself sliding into anger, fear, jealousy or envy.

We can use anger as an example. When anger suddenly rears its vicious temperament stop it in tracks by taking the following steps.

1. Ask yourself to TAKE CHARGE by slowly counting from 10 to 0 before you say or doing something you will regret.
2. Ask yourself if your anger is legitimate. It's possible you have a perfect right to be pissed off. That doesn't mean you go off half-cocked.
3. Ask yourself if the intensity of your anger is in proportion to the actual situation. Even if it is, you gain much more by handling it in a calm, cool manner.
4. Remember you possess the Dynamic Weapons of Rational Selfishness and Mind Power. If you're angry with a Social Altruist or an irrationally selfish person you know what other Dynamic Weapons you need. Ready, Aim, Fire. Now that's an effective way to discharge your anger. And you do it by TAKING CHARGE.

Here's a catchy motivational quote for controlling your anger. *"I TAKE CHARGE of my anger by discharging it."*

If you handle it successfully, the next time you're in a similar situation you will be much more inclined to TAKE CHARGE with a cool head. You will begin believing you're one cool customer. It's much easier to remain positive once you understand that along with giant leaps, many small steps make up the life of the Rationally Selfish Individual. Little things mean a lot.

Escaping the Box of Illusion

If you have already committed to the life of a Rationally Selfish Individual, you know that just letting things happen doesn't work to your benefit. Achieving your DEFINITE PURPOSE in Life demands that you TAKE CHARGE of your thoughts, feelings and actions. Have I mentioned anything about the "open sesame" phrase?

Residing at the bottom of a box of illusion takes very little purposive effort. Escaping it could require you making radical lifestyle changes. Self-defeating behavior doesn't vanish overnight. It takes consistent, rational effort on your part. Studies show that it entails about 21 days of consistent effort to replace a bad habit with a life-enhancing one. Fortunately, you possess your Dynamic Weapons—and you may need all of them to eliminate irrationally selfish behavior. Ready, Aim, Fire.

I recommend when you're finished with this book, you read, re-read and read it again. You can make notes in the margin or open a word doc. and type in any thoughts you may have. Loan the book to a friend or recommend that he or she purchases a copy. When you encourage other people to adopt the Rationally Selfish Life, you're helping yourself. It's rewarding to trade value for value with like-minded individuals. It takes a concerted effort to soar with awareness and reach greatness. Do you think the path might become easier if your family and friends are on the same quest, journey and path as you? Now I admit that might be easier said than done. You can't force anyone to escape the box of illusion. The only person you have control over is you—and you know you can TAKE CHARGE of your thoughts, feelings and actions.

Put Your Dynamic Accelerated Awareness Weapon Into Action

Your Dynamic Accelerated Awareness Weapon will help you conquer many of the so-called intellectual illusions of government, business and society. Do you believe everything a social or economic "expert" tells you? The Rationally Selfish Individual realizes most disseminators of "intellectual" knowledge reside in ivory towers. We proved it in Chapter Four when you fortunately captured your Dynamic Unhampered Capitalism Weapon.

You cannot reach out and seize accelerated awareness if you are not willing to practice it from beginning to end. The irrationally selfish individual floats around in a haze of unawareness. He will claim he's aware, but you know it's an illusion. The impeccable warrior makes awareness a priority. He clearly sees reality. Sure, he might make a mistake, but he's quick to acknowledge it and rethink his previous position. What does the Rationally Selfish Man or Woman do after analyzing the error or miscalculation and discovering a new insight? He or she takes action—deliberate and strategic action. (Do you see the possibility of adding another Dynamic Weapon to your psychological arsenal of attack and self-defense.) You won't see him or her waiting around wondering what's going to occur. Just letting stuff happen isn't to his or her liking.

Whenever you feel your awareness slipping away into a haze of non-reality pull out your Dynamic Accelerated Awareness Weapon and blast away the fog. Make sure you have your other Dynamic Weapons ready as reinforcements.

Word of Warning: Should you ever ignorantly abandon your Dynamic Rational Selfishness Weapon, your other weapons will diminish in efficiency. In fact, you'll be lucky if they work at all because you're ammo will be nothing but duds. Why? Because you exist as the Dynamic Rational Selfishness Weapon—and don't you forget it.

Are you aware of your DEFINITE PURPOSE? Do you know what pumps you up? If irrationally selfish behavior stokes the fires of your passion you have a problem. In the book 'The New Science of Super-Awareness" Bill Harris says *"You can only feel or do something that doesn't serve you if you do it outside your awareness. With enough awareness, though, you'll see what you're creating, as you create it—and, you'll instantly drop what doesn't serve you.*

In fact, with enough awareness you'll know just what to do, and it will become increasingly difficult to feel or do something that sabotages you." That my friend is why the Dynamic Accelerated Awareness Weapon is so important. Can you imagine its potency when used along side the Dynamic Anti-Irrational Selfishness Weapon. When the Rationally Selfish Individual commands these Dynamic Weapons he begins vanquishing Social Altruists and irrationally selfish people.

8 Dynamic Weapons for Conquering Life's Illusions

Conquering Conformity

In our society, anyone not conforming to the increasingly bizarre politically correct crap of Social Altruists, do-gooders and world-improvers gets plastered with the label of a right-winger, tea-bagger, fascist, Nazi, libertarian nut, greedy capitalist, anti-American or anti-social outcast. What's really crazy about it is that these violators of individual rights resort to what psychologists call projection or transference. Social Altruists completely commit to the social philosophies of fascism and Nazism. Doublespeak remains their favorite "intellectual" tool for tricking the masses. Here's an excerpt from my book "7 Destructive Economic Illusions Conquered" demonstrating what their "misleading" terms produce in reality.

1. Positive change = negative change
2. Stimulating the economy = inflation and reduction of wealth
3. Creating jobs = eliminating jobs
4. Saving jobs = eliminating new employment opportunities
5. To big to fail = penalizing profitable business, preventing new business creation
6. Easy credit = more debt and malinvestments
7. Beneficial regulations = more restrictions on your personal liberty and freedom

If we wanted to get crude about it we could call them lying sacks of sh--. Time to pull out your Dynamic Anti-Social Altruism Weapon. Ready, Aim, Fire.

If you've fallen for the fallacies of Social Altruists it's because you don't possess the awareness to see through illusion. I understand how difficult life becomes when you stumble through it not knowing where you're going, what you're doing or where you fit into the scheme of existence. If that's the case, don't let it bother you. I was so unaware when I was younger, that I didn't even know I was unaware. I wasn't conscious enough to conform to social conventions. I guess in a way you can say I was lucky. I sure learned a lot through woe instead of wisdom. I'm glad I wised up. Right now I can firmly state that if I can gain awareness so can you.

We need to supply a good definition of conformity.

Conformity: behavior in accordance with socially accepted conventions or standards.

I don't know about you, but I find that definition totally uninspiring. You might as well exist as a automatic response device. If you do, I guarantee Social Altruists will love you to death.

Social Altruists hope and pray that you accept their illusions without giving them any thought. They expect you to mindlessly conform to their politically correct platform of propaganda, BS, half-truths and downright lies. These mental, emotional and spiritual parasites fear the Rationally Selfish Individual who lives for his own sake. The Social Altruist expects you to relinquish your highest values for whatever snake oil he offers in return. When you refuse, expect him to resort to an ad hominem attack. You might ask what kind of attack is that. Let's allow dictionary.reference.com to supply a definition.

ad hominem
adjective
1. appealing to one's prejudices, emotions, or special interests rather than to one's intellect or reason.
2. attacking and opponent's character rather than answering his argument.

We already know the Rationally Selfish Individual won't abandon his intellect or reason. How about an attack on his character? Well, you don't want engage in an argument with anyone who refuses to use logical arguments. Instead, you pull out your Dynamic Weapons and let him know that his influence over you is non-existent. Then you allow your Dynamic Weapons to do the talking. Can you imagine a Social Altruist standing up to a Rationally Selfish Individual.

The Rationally Selfish Individual Handles Adversity

How do you react:

1. If your car breaks down?
2. If you hate your job because your boss is always on your case?
3. If you lose your job?
4. If you begin experiencing financial problems?
5. If your boyfriend or girlfriend says something you don't like?
6. If your significant other or spouse cheats on you?
7. If your significant other wants to break up with you?
8. If your spouse asks for a divorce?
9. If your children misbehave?
10. If your teenager acts out of control?
11. If you just feel out of whack?
12. If you're having a bad day?

No doubt we could add hundreds of questions to the above. I don't expect you to be thrilled with any of the adversities I mentioned. In fact, it's natural to feel some dismay and emotional pain. Losing gainful employment creates a stressful situation. Suffering a broken heart gives you a crushing, sinking feeling. The devastation from losing a loved one remains indescribable. It's understandable if you sink into a temporary state of depression and cry your eyes out. However, if you breakdown into a non-functioning state or begin indulging in irrationally selfish behavior, you've lost control. A Rationally Selfish Individual will regain control of his thoughts feelings and action. Your Dynamic Weapons will see you through adversity. Hopefully, you also have valuable friends and family to help you get over your trials and tribulations.

Life presents you with annoyances that finally get on your nerves. It's like the Chinese Water Torture Process that's supposed to drive its victims insane. Each little annoying occurrence drives you closer and closer to losing your cool. Finally a seemingly inconsequential event causes you to explode into a fit of emotional rage. In a heartbeat, you're reduced to the status of an irrationally selfish person. Your destructive words and actions cause a personal or professional relationship to fall and break like a valuable Ming Vase. In addition you deplete your positive energy. You're completely washed out. I hate to say it but I used to do that. Fortunately for me and those around me that was long ago.

I don't blame you if you don't value the opinions of Social Altruists and irrationally selfish people. I mentioned the scenario of a boss who's on your case. If he's belongs to one of the classes just mentioned you need to get the hell out of there ASAP. Frank J. Rumbauskas, Jr. of "Never Cold Call" fame says *"I never accept second-class behavior from any person. I walk away from anyone who disrespects me."* That sounds like a code of the impeccable warrior.

You can expect Social Altruists and irrationally selfish people to judge you using floating abstractions and a faulty moral code. You know the Rationally Selfish Individual will realistically judge you by your thoughts, feelings and actions. Your behavior says it all. If you leave home without your Dynamic Rational Selfishness Weapon he will immediately see that you're walking around naked. Should you suddenly discover that you're disrobing at an inappropriate time, the Dynamic Weapons of Mind Power and Accelerated Awareness will prevent you from making a serious mistake. By the way, we're closing in on some powerful ammo.

Crime and Loss of Self-Respect

Irrationally selfish people eventually lose their pride, honor and self-respect. You can't expect to retain these when you live a second-handed existence. The unfortunate individual usually wanders through life combining negative emotions with self-defeating behavior. A stale mediocrity is the best he or she can expect. Often failure and frustration gain the upper hand. In a worse case scenario his lack of self respect results in him turning to crime.

When it comes to crime, you must understanding the difference between irrationally selfish people and Social Altruists. The former lose all self-respect, allowing their values to sink into an abyss of moral sewage. Social Altruists have no self-respect to lose because they're sociopaths. It's irrelevant because they're devoid of any normal human feelings. In addition, they use "moral values" as power plays to enlarge their gigantic egos. Are you familiar with Freud's superego? According to Encyclopaedia Britannica *"The superego is the ethical component of the personality and provides the moral standards by which the ego operates. The superego's criticisms, prohibitions, and inhibitions form a person's conscience, and its positive aspirations and ideals represent one's idealized self-image, or ego ideal."* Do you get the the part about ethical component of personality? It appears Social Altruists shutdown their superego—that is if they had one. Damn! I think I see a Social Altruist on the horizon. Time to unleash my Dynamic Anti-Social Altruism Weapon. Ready, Aim, Fire and repeat.

You're probably thinking "You definitely exposed Social Altruists as having a criminal mind. How are they different than irrationally selfish people who turn to crime." That's a good question.

It's time to repeat an iron law of human action. All people act in what they believe to be their own best interest. There are no exceptions. Everyone acts from selfishness.

The irrationally selfish man or woman believe he acts from self-interest when he decides to satisfy his or her desires with criminal activity. That's obviously an illusion, because self-defeating criminal behavior gets bad results—like a term in the penitentiary. Social Altruists are savvy enough to express their criminal tendencies in legal activities. You gotta believe they love interventionistic governments that stomp on individual rights. These sociopaths probably love abusive governments more than they love irrationally selfish people. Of course, their "love" is unrecognizable to the compassionate heart.

The evil of a Social Altruist know no bounds. He will use the government's apparatus of violent compulsion and coercion to transform honest citizens into criminals. He thrills at the thought of criminalizing the Rationally Selfish Individual. The more laws restricting voluntary exchanges the better. In fact it's beneficial to liberty-violators if the legal code far surpasses your ability to comprehend it. These dangerous enemies of life, liberty and property rights certainly prefer that nothing should be pure, clear-cut or honest. My god! What horrible bastards! Time to get out your Dynamic Weapons and start blasting away. Damn, they're enough to make a Rationally Selfish Individual lose his head. Remember, we must remain calm. cool and collected—always.

The impeccable warrior doesn't sacrifice tomorrow for today unless his immediate survival is at stake. The great free market economist Ludwig von Mises stated *"It may sometimes be expedient for a man to heat the stove with his furniture. But he should not delude himself by believing that he has discovered a wonderful new method of heating his premises."* The irrationally selfish person burns his "furniture" day in and day out until Social Altruists come to the rescue with more wood to burn. Can you guess whose "furniture" these criminals pilfered in order to come up with the "wood." I think you know. Ready, Aim, Fire. Hey, that's some mighty nice shooting.

As a Rationally Selfish Individual you enjoy today, but plan for tomorrow. You know tomorrow matters because your DEFINITE PURPOSE fires you up with a burning desire to achieve it. The only thing better than tomorrow is today and the only thing better than today is right now. Now that's exciting. You piece together your marvelous journey through life with your moment by moment successes and failures. Remember what we learned about failure. You can let failure mock you or you can allow it to supply you the seeds of success. In Galatians 6:7 of the King James Version of the Bible we learn *"Be not deceived; God is not mocked: for whatsoever a man soweth, that shall he also reap."*

The Taste of the Forbidden Fruit

You will be tempted to taste the forbidden fruit—time after time. Fortunately you know how to distinguish between Rationally Selfish Behavior and irrationally selfish behavior. It's possible a "temptation" might correspond to your highest values but be out of style or old-fashioned. You might be afraid of what other people will think of you or you might even fear your peers will laugh at you. You should know by now that the impeccable warrior refuses to live by second-hand values. He decides what's right or wrong. For our purposes we will consider the taste of the forbidden fruit temptations irrationally selfish people succumb to.

You might have noticed that I capitalize Social Altruist(s) and Social Altruism. These terms are ideal types although that might seem like a misnomer. In addition, you need to realize that these liberty violators remain worthy opponents, although the term worthy might seem like a contradiction. Do I have to tell you why I capitalize Rational Selfishness and Rationally Selfish Individual and refuse to capitalize irrational selfishness and irrationally selfish?

Self-destructive short-term pleasures often feel good. I've heard that an injection of heroin supplies the user an incredible euphoria. It's been reported that smoking crack is pure sensuous stimulation. An irrationally selfish person looking for kicks will eagerly eat from the forbidden fruit.

A Rationally Selfish Individual wouldn't consider going near the sweet but poisonous fruit. He loves the pleasures of the body, mind and spirit; however he enjoys activities that enhance his being. There's art, music, fine wine or good liquor consumed in moderation, loving sex, nature, physical, mental and metaphysical activities and anything else you can think of that brings you happiness and joy without endangering your well-being.

Let's say you slip up, put on your irrationally selfish persona and partake in the forbidden fruit. It's possible you more than taste it, you go on a gluttonous binge. Before you know it you feel mentally, emotionally, physically and spiritually sick. In fact, you're lower than a snake's belly. Didn't Jed Clampett say that? Anyway, what do you do now?

You know you're on a very slippery slope. Irrationally selfish people form bad habits as easy as 1,2,3. The forbidden fruit imprisons them in a world of illusion. Do you want to live like this or do you escape before it's too late. I have a question. Where in the hell are your Dynamic Weapons? It's appears that when you leave home without your Dynamic Rational Selfishness Weapon you suddenly become afflicted with amnesia. Remember you wield the Dynamic Weapon and you exist as the Dynamic Weapon—and don't you forget it. The answer to the question in the previous paragraph is you once again TAKE CHARGE of your thoughts, feelings and actions. You think, feel and act as an impeccable warrior thinks, feels and acts. You stand tall as a Rationally Selfish Individual.

Honesty and Integrity

Once a person adopts irrational selfishness as a permanent life style, he separates from a virtue know as integrity. He fixates on short-term pleasures and benefits to the exclusion of his intermediate or long-term well-being. He (she) prefers something for nothing. If he spirals out of control he would prefer to steal something instead of working for it. The lyrics from the song "Stealin'" sung by Uriah Heap says it all. *"I made my break and a big mistake stealin' when I should've been buyin'."* Once you break away from Rational Selfishness and descend into irrational selfishness you can say goodbye to honesty and integrity.

Do you like to do business with someone devoid honesty and integrity. Even irrationally selfish people prefer not to be cheated or ripped off. Since they live in a world of illusion and unwittingly adopt second-hand values they're vulnerable to the unsubstantiated claims of Social Altruists, sociopaths and petty con men.

Is there a gray area between Rational Selfishness and irrational selfishness? Is it possible to alternate between the two? I'm going to hit you with the truth. You cannot successfully move back and forth between two diametrically opposed lifestyles because bad habits are easier to form than good habits. The irrationally selfish person unconsciously and easily attracts bad habits. Good habits take awareness and conscious effort. That's why I supplied you with the Dynamic Accelerated Awareness Weapon. You're a person of integrity, so whenever you're tempted to indulge in the forbidden fruit you quickly pull out your fire power. Ready, Aim, Fire.

Do you believe irrational selfishness can actually be a sustainable lifestyle? I guess it's possible for the irrationally selfish person to stumble through life with his self-defeating behavior. He might even capture some success. Let's say he (she) develops skills in some areas of his life. He may even have some inborn qualities he inherited from his ancestors. You've seen entertainers, sports figures and other public celebrities display amazing talents, only to fall hard because of their irrationally selfish behavior. Just envision the long-term success these individuals would have achieved had they lived the Rationally Selfish Life. It's tragic to witness someone trade a piece of his honesty and integrity for a cheap thrill. Eventually he runs out of his virtuous currency.

The Rationally Selfish Individual firmly believes in unhampered capitalism (free enterprise). Because he acts from honesty and integrity, he's committed to discovering cause and effect relationships in the sphere of human action (economics). The last thing he needs is Social Altruists tricking him into accepting fallacious and destructive economic policies. He opposes socialism and government interventionism, spurious social systems that encourage people to want something for nothing. That's why I supplied you the Dynamic Unhampered Capitalism Weapon. For your benefit I wrote a short book titled "7 Destructive Economic Illusions Conquered." Yes, I'm dedicated to helping you conquer personal and economic illusions. Your personal liberty and economic freedom depends on it.

The Rationally Selfish Individual respects a person's life, liberty and property. He firmly believes in individual rights. He knows you don't deal with fellow humans as slaves or fodder to satisfy irrational desires. He loves to trade value for value. That's what you call honesty and integrity.

Wisely he resists mass movements because these are usually based on fallacious economic and social theories, unfocused thinking and emotionalism. In most case, their unstated policies would extract wealth from productive people which amounts to eating the seed corn. In addition, they sit on shaky foundations of failed institutional models. Imagine supporting programs that are designed to keep hapless men and women beaten down. It's unthinkable. I know you don't want to give up your individuality and join a Mobocracy. You stand strong and courageous as an impeccable warrior, the Rationally Selfish Individual.

Moving Forward by Letting Go of the Past

I mentioned how easy it is to regress back to irrational selfishness. When you shed your Rational Selfishness persona and foolishly wander around without your most powerful Dynamic Weapon, temptation relentlessly stalks you. To make matters worse you forget about your other Dynamic Weapons which leaves you completely defenseless. You might wonder why you would act so recklessly. It has to do with past negative influences.

It's possible you suffered from some trauma or unpleasant occurrences during your formative development years between the age of 3 and 7. You probably don't remember a lot of it, but it's firmly entrenched in the subconscious mind. Incredibly you act from subconscious desires and don't even know it. Suddenly self-defeating thoughts and feelings lead to actions that sabotage your quest to achieve your goals and desires. Sadly, your DEFINITE PURPOSE vanishes somewhere in the mist of irrationally selfish behavior. What are you to do.?

It's hard to admit that you suffer from mental and emotional scars that keep you from living the life you desire. In addition it's easy to blame your parents or other authority figures for your failures and frustrations. To make matters worse, you still feel anger for some of the trauma your peers, authority figures and parents inflicted on you during your adolescence and pre-adolescence years. Intellectually, you know a Rationally Selfish Individual TAKES CHARGE of his thoughts, feelings and actions. You do pretty good most of the time but every so often someone or a difficult circumstance pushes your buttons causing you to reel out of control. I understand. It used to happen to me. Fortunately, I moved forward by letting go of the past. Every once in a while I feel like spiraling out of control and striking out at my "enemies." I make sure I TAKE CHARGE of my thoughts, feelings and actions. I terminate self-defeating behavior. It's a privilege to own a psychological arsenal of attack and self-defense.

Here's something I've said before. There's no such thing as perfection in the sphere of human action so don't beat yourself up for being imperfect. The best you can do is consistently move towards perfection—and that's a lifetime endeavor. Your burning desire to achieve your DEFINITE PURPOSE in Life should spur you on to greatness.

How do you let go of the past? You possess 2 Dynamic Weapons that will assist you in your efforts to diminish the effect past negative events have on your life. Do you know which ones I'm talking about? Yes, it's time to resort to the Dynamic Weapons of Mind Power and Expanded

Awareness. I am ready to supply you their most potent ammo—that is if you will accept it.

Powerful Ammo for Mind Power and Expanded Awareness

I would appreciate it if you would allow yourself to open up your mind to what I'm about to reveal. Actually, you should be the one to feel gratitude and appreciate for the enormous gift I'm offering you. All you have to do is hold out your hand and accept it, but first you must travel to a place where it's available.

In the book "7 Powerful Steps for Conquering Life's Illusions" I stated "Some Objectivists disdain anything they can't prove through deductive or inductive reasoning. If you're familiar with Ayn Rand's teachings, I don't have to tell you her fervent followers have an aversion to mysticism. Of course, when it comes to social issues, resorting to mysticism results in all the disasters she so eloquently describes in "Atlas Shrugged." In fact, during the continuous economic decline Atlas may very well shrug. You may have noticed that Ayn Rand's teachings heavily influence me. After all, she presents an integrated, logical philosophical system."

You probably wonder where I'm going with this. It's possible I'm taking you to a place you've never been before. If you've visited this enlightening dimension of the mind then you know where the journey begins and delightfully continues. You certainly don't want the pleasures and ecstasies of life to end before it's time to move on.

Maybe you're skeptical. Allow me to introduce you to some wisdom I discovered in the marvelous newsletter "Laissez Faire Today." In the book "The Art of Contrary Thinking" Neill Humphrey says *"Thrust your thoughts out of a rut. In a word, be a nonconformist when using your mind. Sameness of thinking is a natural attribute. So you must expect to practice a little to get into the habit of throwing your mind into directions that are opposite to the obvious. Obvious thinking — or thinking the same way in which everyone else is thinking — commonly leads to wrong judgments and wrong conclusions."*

The Ammo of Meditation

In order to operate at maximum efficiency, your Dynamic Weapons of Mind Power and Expanded Awareness require the ammo of meditation. If the idea of meditation bothers you, you can substitute its sister ammo reflection. If you really want to oust the demons of the mind you can use both meditation and reflection.

Let's say you're a Christian. Prayer and meditation go together hand in hand. Here's an insight from Joshua 1:8 King James Version *"This book of the law shall not depart out of thy mouth; but thou shalt **meditate** therein day and night, that thou mayest observe to do according to all that is written therein: for then thou shalt make thy way prosperous, and then thou shalt have good success. "*

Matthew 6:6 King James Version of the New Testament perfectly describes meditation from a Christian point of view. *"But thou, when thou prayest, enter into thy closet, and when thou hast shut thy door, pray to thy Father which is in secret; and thy Father which seeth in secret shall reward thee openly."*

Attention Objectivists: I will firmly state that I know you can increase your power of reason while you're in a relaxed state of mind which means you become more efficient at integrating concepts.

I hope I proved that anyone can receive benefits from meditation. Let's explore the truth about one of the most pleasurable and rewarding activities you can indulge in. You know your Dynamic Weapons conquer life's illusions. They also defend you against those who attempt to strip you of your personal liberty and economic freedom. In addition they enhance the pleasures of the body, mind and spirit. Now it's time to supply you with some ammo of ecstasy.

Illusions and Myths about Meditation

I would like to explode some illusions and myths about meditation. Meditation doesn't require you to become an ascetic monk and live a life of self-sacrifice and self-denial. It doesn't mean that you abandon all concerns about human affairs by becoming a spiritual guru—meditating all of your waking hours while your disciples take care of your physical needs. If you fall for that illusion you've crossed over into Social Altruism. Where's your Dynamic Anti-Social Altruism Weapon when you need it.

You don't abandon reason in order to discover spiritual insights. If the day arrives when you realize you can transcend all the laws of physics and praxeology, you've unwisely jumped off a cliff without the parachute of your Dynamic Rational Selfishness Weapon.

Let's say that during a period of extended meditation you make an important discovery. You suddenly realized that inflation could be stopped in its tracks through selective wage and price controls. And you were really blessed during this meditation—because you discovered a method where the Federal Reserve System could stimulate the economy through the creation of more paper money without the effects of rising prices, economic distortions and transfers of wealth from Main Street to Wall Street. It looks like your Dynamic Unhampered Capitalism Weapon flew the coop. Maybe its existence was just an illusion.

Another example is that you believed you developed the power to astral travel during your meditation. You can leap tall buildings like Superman. Now I'm not denying this is possible in a deep state of meditation. The mind can be creative and imaginative. However, if you came out of your meditative state and believed you wore Superman's cape, you would be suffering under an extreme case of illusion (insanity)—and quite possibly discover if death is an illusion, a reality or neither.

Books such as the "Life and Teachings of Masters of the Far East" series report such occurrences as if they were fact. Maybe I'm just being narrow-minded with my skepticism. On second thought, I'm thinking as an impeccable warrior thinks. Isn't it more likely these stories of great feats are meant to encourage you to accomplish more in your life? The series of books encouraged me to see through illusion—and overcome my limitations.

Now that being said, here is a list of some of the benefits you will receive from daily meditation. There are many studies that support the life-enhancing advantages I am providing you.

1. Lower heart rate.

2. Lowered levels of cortisol and lactate which reduces stress.
3. Reduced cholesterol levels.
4. Decreased blood pressure. High blood pressure can cause erectile dysfunction which definitely could interfere with your enjoyment of the important pleasure of loving sex.
5. Higher levels of DHEAS in senior citizens which is a sign of youthfulness. Ah, to be physically, mentally and sexually active in the twilight of your years.
6. Greater creativity. Adding creativity to your Rationally Selfish lifestyle rewards you with a tremendous variety of empowering experiences.
7. Decreased depression. It's difficult to enjoy life if you're down and out.
8. Increased feelings of vitality and rejuvenation. To feel eternally youthful is a blessing you don't want to live without.
9. Increased happiness. Isn't happiness pretty much the end game of life?
10. An increased power of reasoning. You will develop the ability to integrate concepts more efficiently.

I want to thank Dr. Joan Borysenko for pointing out the many benefits of meditation. I hope you understand why you want to endow your Dynamic Weapons of Mind Power and Accelerated Awareness with the potent ammo of meditation. It also works well with your other Dynamic Weapons.

The Spiritual Benefits of Meditation

A discussion of the many religious, spiritual and metaphysical systems remain out of the parameters of this book. In addition, I'm not attempting to start any philosophical or religious arguments. My goal is to supply you the Dynamic Weapons that assist you in conquering life's illusions. I've read books on Christianity (traditional and New Age) Buddhism (Zen), Hinduism, the Kabbalah, Objectivism, etc. Many of them are quite good. Two of my favorites are The Bible (King James Version) and Atlas Shrugged. Now let's get on to the spiritual benefits of meditation

Many people meditate for the spiritual benefits and this is where you receive an abundance of rewarding experiences. Your sixth sense kicks in—giving you the awareness to avoid activities that smack of irrational selfishness. "The small voice within" guides you in moments of need.

To be spiritually attuned to "all there is" adds a special flavor to your life. People refer to "all there is" as God, Universal Mind, Allah, Infinite Intelligence, Nothingness, Zero, the Big Bang etc. Use whatever word(s) unleashes your spiritual feelings. For our purposes I will call "all their is" God. If you play video games and decide you're sick of getting killed or you just want to go on a rampage without danger, you access the cheat code called the "god mode."

I believe God is the original cause and the source of "all there is." Hey, that's similar to your Dynamic Rational Selfishness Weapon. You wield it and you are it. I guess you could say that God and the Universe are synonymous. Whatever you believe is perfectly acceptable. Since meditation is your personal experience with the Universal Source you can draw your own conclusions.

By the way being an Atheist doesn't preclude you from meditating to obtain accelerated awareness. **Profound Insight:** You just discovered that the ammo of meditation leads you to your Dynamic Accelerated Awareness Weapon. Now that's a conundrum. You seek something you already have. Anyway, I'm sure you realize there's probably an ultimate first cause for all that exists. You may refer to call it the "Big Bang" or some other scientific term. You can also meditate on "a priori" concepts or axiomatic concepts if you prefer. I obtain many benefits meditating on the "a priori" categories of human action—such as causality.

Achieving a state of oneness with the universe and all of its marvelous expressions creates richer and more intense experiences. You savor every bite of food because you are aware of the process of eating. Your sense of taste develops an acuteness that enhances your satisfaction in drinking beverages. The sip of fine wine or Extra Smooth Brandy becomes truly divine.

When you listen to good music your enjoyment is delightfully expansive because your sensitivity has increased. Your emotions soar to heavenly levels of joy.

When you make love with your partner—and it is making love not just sex—you both experience an intensity most don't realize. Your body, mind and spirit create pleasures that irrationally selfish men and women can only dream about. You know about the Social Altruists craze (or should we say craziness) for equality. Is it possible these "crazies" might consider passing a law that all sexual experiences must be equal? You know which Dynamic Weapon you need. Ready, Aim, Fire. Ready, Aim, Fire. Reload when necessary.

All areas of your life become more enjoyable because you spiritually tune in to the universe and all of its various expressions.

You also gain greater control over your thoughts, feelings and actions—which translates into a powerful control over your life. You integrate the hemispheres of your brain far more effectively. The impeccable warrior, the Rationally Selfish Individual makes his plans, puts them into action and accomplishes them. Could it get any more exciting than this? You're loading your Dynamic Weapons of Mind Power and Accelerated Awareness with the spice of life.

If you currently meditate you know where I'm coming from. If you're meditating and not receiving all the marvelous benefits I described then read on.

Time to Take a Journey to Accelerated Awareness

It's time to take a journey that transforms your Dynamic Accelerated Awareness Weapon into a force to be reckoned with. Let the voyage begin.

1. Sit in a relaxing position. It's up to you whether you sit in a comfortable recliner or on the floor in a lotus position. Some people like the floor or even the ground outdoors because they feel connected to Mother Earth. I've done quite well sitting comfortably in a chair.
2. Eliminate all distractions. Make sure you turn off your cell phone or mute it. You may want to set the alarm on it in order to time your meditation. That way you will be able to float into

relaxation without the fear of going over your designated time limit.
3. Gently close your eyes. It will be difficult to relax if you squeeze them shut. You want to transform your meditation experience into a natural event.
4. Breathe in deeply through your nose and hold it in at least 3 seconds. Make sure your intake of air travels all the way down to your stomach. You will know your doing it right because your stomach will expand.
5. Exhale slowly out of your mouth. You're not forcing the air out of your lungs. You are gently expelling it.
6. Continuing the breathing exercise until your body feels relaxed. You can also still each part of your body individually. Feel the release of tension from your toes, feet, legs, thighs, stomach, chest, arms, hands, fingers, shoulders, neck, face and crown.
7. Visualize an object such as a candle flame and concentrate on it. Do not force your concentration, but allow it to occur freely and easily. You can also chant a mantra such as AH, AUM or OM. If chanting seems like mystical nonsense—concentrate on an axiomatic concept such as existence.
8. If possible let go of all thoughts. If your mind drifts bring it back. It's perfectly acceptable to briefly experience your thoughts, however, allow them to gently float on by. You accept them, then release them. **Note:** If you're using meditation to reflect on an area of your life, solve a problem, program the subconscious or to pray, you might want to allow your mind to access pertinent information. You can also repeat affirmations. In some cases, it's necessary for you to concentrate on the issue at hand.
9. Continue to release all tension and negative thoughts from your being. Sometimes it helpful to imagine a white light surrounding you, dissolving blocks and obstacles.
10. Through slow, natural breathing and relaxation you'll be able to achieve a state of peace. Don't stress out if this doesn't happen at first or it doesn't occur all the time. Often inner conflicts rise to the surface. Experience them completely then let em' go. If it's too painful you can discontinue your meditation and try it

another time.
11. Eventually you will experience the euphoria of oneness with God, universe or existence. Melding with "all there is" won't happen overnight—although you never know. Accept your meditation adventure for what it is.
12. You end your voyage by slowly counting from 1 to 5. Spend a few minutes or more reflecting on your journey. Now it's time to fully live in reality—and that means taking action, then more action. Your DEFINITE PURPOSE in Life depends on it.

I admit this takes some practice. You should see some immediate benefits. Other benefits may take longer.

I meditate anywhere from an hour to an hour and a half per day. You can receive great benefits from meditating only 24 minutes a day. This is equivalent to one minute for every hour of the day. If you want to meditate longer that is fine.

I didn't mention the chakras. MindBodyGreen says "There are 7 main energy centers in the body, known as chakras. Each chakra is located throughout our body so that it correlates to specific body ailment and physical dysfunctions; each energy center also houses our mental and emotional strengths. When we have a physical issue, it creates weaknesses in our emotional behavior. When we release the stale energy from the body, it can undo any tightness, stiffness, or malfunction of that area."

Finding the Time to Meditate

Looking back over my own life and some of the difficult challenges I faced, I can say with certainty that meditation excels as one of the most important paths to practicing Rational Selfishness. It's the type of ammo that repels irrational selfishness

You may be asking yourself "When will I find the time to meditate. You're telling me to invest almost an hour a day. Where am I going to find another hour?"

I found out that meditation increases my energy and efficiency so much that I accomplish more in less time. I estimate that for every hour

I meditate, I gain three more hours to pursue my DEFINITE PURPOSE and enjoy the pleasures of the body, mind and spirit. That's quite a bargain. You trade one hour to gain three hours.

If you meditate for just 24 minutes per day you gain 72 minutes for a total of an extra 48 minutes per day. Imagine what you can do with that bonus of time. DEFINITE PURPOSE in Life and pleasures of the body, mind and spirit here I come.

Another benefit of meditation is your sleep needs decrease. I prefer to meditate first thing in the morning. I feel so good after my journey that I'm able to go full speed—and I have plenty of time and energy to do what I want to do—my way.

Get up an hour earlier if necessary. Wouldn't you love to live the life you always dreamed of? Invest at least an hour a day in yourself. It's well worth it. You happily load your Dynamic Weapons of Mind Power and Accelerated Awareness with the Dynamic Ammo of Meditation. That's Dynamic Ammo for your Dynamic Weapons. Isn't it amazing that your psychological arsenal hold armaments of peace and harmony.

Recommended Meditation Tools

How would you like to accelerate your progress? I recommend purchasing some tapes or CD's to help you learn how to meditate. You can go to any metaphysical book and record store and find an audio set for beginning meditators. If there is a Half Price book store in your area there's a good chance you can discover it—at a good price.

If you are serious about receiving all the benefits from meditation including the spiritual, I have an important recommendation. Purchase Jonathan Parker's "Pathways to Mastership" course. It is second to none. It's one of my prized possessions.

If you have been meditating for years and are still experiencing difficulties in your life, I highly recommend Holosync. Bill Harris created a headphone series that helps you meditate like a monk and experience lasting changes in your life. Visit the Centerpointe Research Institute and discover a revolutionary tool for accelerated awareness and self-change. Beginning meditators will also benefit from Holosync.

Conclusion

You just captured the Dynamic Accelerated Awareness Weapon along with the incredibly powerful ammo of meditation. You now possess 6 Dynamic Weapons in your psychological arsenal of attack and self-defense.

1. Anti-Social Altruism
2. Anti-Irrational Selfishness
3. Rational Selfishness
4. Unhampered Capitalism
5. Mind Power
6. Accelerated Awareness

Remember that you not only possess the Dynamic Rational Selfishness Weapon, you exist as the Dynamic Weapon. If you forget it, you will be shooting duds. Now it's time to capture your 7th Dynamic Weapon.

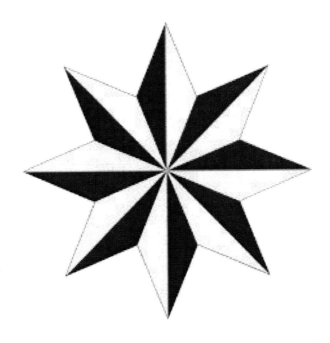

Imagine for a moment that it is possible for you to experience the joy of your existence, no matter what is happening around you. The Dynamic Joy of Existence Weapon protects you from your own self-defeating conscious and subconscious thoughts and feelings. It allows you to express pleasure, ecstasy and happiness.

CHAPTER EIGHT

DYNAMIC JOY OF EXISTENCE WEAPON

Do you fall for the illusion that Social Altruists want to see you happy and independent? As a Rationally Selfish Individual, you destroyed that dangerous chimera with your Dynamic Weapons. If for some reason, you haven't obliterated Social Altruism, it's time to go back to start and reread Chapter One.

It's hard to face the fact that irrationally selfish people hate to see you experience the joy of your existence. Your happiness brings out their negative feelings of envy, jealousy—and hatred. That's really sad. Social Altruists fear it because it indicates you don't need them. These purveyors of human misery prefer victims who they can continuously victimize. Your joy, your happiness, your independence makes them want to destroy you. Their favorite weapon to severely hamper your efforts to improve your well-being is the violent compulsion and coercion of the government. Ayn Rand's masterpiece "Atlas Shrugged" reveals their evil ways. Let's hear from Ayn Rand's Rationally Selfish hero of logic and reason, John Galt.

"Sweep aside those hatred-eaten mystics (Social Altruists), who pose as friends of humanity and preach that the highest virtue man can practice is to hold his own life as of no value. Do they tell you that the purpose of morality is to curb man's instinct of self-preservation? It is for the purpose of self-preservation that man needs a code of morality. The only man who desires to be moral is the man who desires to live."

Rational Selfishness reigns as a life-enhancing code of morality for the individual who wants to live a truly human existence.

Incredibly Social Altruists deny that A is A. Oh, they won't explicitly tell you this. But their anti-life philosophy of selflessness and self-sacrifice confirms it. John Galt sets us straight.

"Are you seeking to know what is wrong with the world? All the disasters that have wrecked your world, came from your leaders' attempt to evade the fact that A is A. All the secret evil you dread to face within you and all the pain you have ever endured, came from your own attempt

to evade the fact that A is A."

Our Dynamic Weapons protect us from the enemies of personal liberty and economic freedom. They also smoke out the varmints of illusion that reside in our own consciousness.

A Day in a Life of an Irrationally Selfish Person

You have to feel some compassion for an irrationally selfish person. Perhaps you're struggling with your negative emotions or you once allowed them to victimize you. I don't know about you but I battled irrational selfishness for a long time. Of course, I was missing quite a few Dynamic Weapons. Fortunately, you're getting the opportunity to benefit from my experience. You've heard the expression "Walk a mile in my shoes." You don't always know what another person has gone through. Life presents you trials and tribulations that challenge even the strongest individual, so let's go through life with some love and understanding—with our Dynamic Weapons ready for action when needed. It's time for us to experience a day in a life of the irrationally selfish person. I hope it's not too painful.

"That damn alarm clock is my worst enemy. I just wish it would shut up and let me slip back into slumber. Now I have to drag myself out of bed and shut it off. How I hate facing another day. I'm so tired and I feel down and out. I just thought of something. My work associate Jim is coming over to party tonight. He says he will bring a bottle of Southern Comfort. At least I have that to look forward to.

I wish he would also bring a couple of hot chicks over. My last girlfriend said I was too pessimistic and wasn't any fun. I thought we were having a good time drinking, listening to some music and drinking some more. Come to think it over, the last time she was here I couldn't "get it up." She told me I wasn't much good for anything except maybe drinking. I haven't seen her since. Anyway, she was one selfish bitch.

I hate my job, but what else can I do. I can't think of any kind of work that would amuse me. Oh well, I guess work isn't supposed to be fun. Still, there must be some kind of purpose in all of this, but I don't know-----. Thinking about all of this confuses me. Didn't someone say it isn't good to think too much.

Well, I better get ready and drag myself off to work before I lose my job. The boss told me I better shape up or else. He even wrote me up for something that wasn't my fault. He claims he told me to update the virus and anti-spyware protection on our company's computers. I don't remember anything about. I did notice the one I was using was dragging ass. I kinda liked it because I could move slower and not stress out, although I wouldn't want my personal laptop to do that. It would be kinda hard to watch porn flicks if they kept freezing up. Anyway, how was I to know it was about ready to permanently crash. He even harassed me by asking how come I didn't see the renewal notices. What an asshole! Why's everybody always picking on me?"

I don't think we need to go into the rest of the day. It doesn't get any better.

A festering neurosis hampers the irrationally selfish person. He bounces around in various stages of misery, unhappiness and short-term "pleasures." Finally he consciously or subconsciously adopts a tragic sense of life.

I'm not talking about people who are suffering temporary sorrow because of loss or trauma. I'm referring to hapless individuals who have accepted negativity, sorrow and pessimism as a way of life.

Often you can't avoid an irrationally selfish person. Here's a major reason why you don't want to deal with him or her minus you Dynamic Weapons. You would think that miserable people would desire to be around happy individuals hoping some of it would rub off on them. Well, don't believe it. Unfortunately, I used to think that. We'll skip the gory details of my excursions into an alien world where "A" is anything but "A" and 1+ 1 never equals 2. Understand that neurotics envy your happiness and often secretly hate you for it. Shockingly, it is possible that they secretly wish for your demise. The dark, murky color of their malevolent sense of life blackens out the rainbow colors of the joy of existence.

A Day in a Life of a Rationally Selfish Individual

I wrote an article called "A Day in a Life of the Lady Libertarian

Warrior." Here's a woman who discovered Rational Selfishness and captured the joy of her existence. Let's allow her to enlighten us.

"During my morning meditation, my mind alternated between sublime thoughts of beauty and the all-encompassing bliss of stillness. Delightfully, I receive much enlightenment and euphoria from the quiet of my universal connection. However, some of my most profound moments arrive when I feel the ecstasy of my body, mind and spirit. Ever since my discovery that I can control my thoughts, feelings and actions, I experience pleasure and ecstasy on a daily basis. No longer do I suffer as I once did. I think the biggest surprise of my life is how much I've grown spiritually and intellectually. I guess you can call me a Lady Warrior.

Since it is Saturday, many people are enjoying an afternoon of leisure. As I walk around the neighborhood on a clear, sunny day, I connect with everything around me. The deep blue of the dreamy sky makes me feel I could reach the heights of an eagle or a jet airliner. At one time, I would have walked along lost in thoughts that scattered in every direction, oblivious to my surroundings. Since I discovered my warriorship, I am sensitive to what I see, smell, hear, feel and touch. I thrill to all of my experiences.

I love my off days, but I also love my work. Today is a wonderful day, but so are the days I am producing values. It seems the better I feel about life, my experiences and those around me, the more enjoyable my work becomes. I receive great satisfaction from it.

I realize that I exist to discover and live my highest values. The euphoric feeling I receive from living my life as an impeccable warrior remains with me most of the time. I experience the joy of my existence because I think, feel and act as a warrior thinks, feels and acts. Do you know how to achieve oneness? Well, it happens when you integrate the body, mind and spirit. It's an illusion to believe you are separated from all there is."

You can see how your thoughts and feeling set the tone for the day. As a Rationally Selfish Individual you wake up with your Dynamic Weapons of Mind Power and Accelerated Awareness. Meditating in the morning immediately loads them with powerful ammo. You pursue your DEFINITE PURPOSE in Life with a passion. Do you know your passion is contagious. You will be able to light up other people with your fire and enthusiasm. You might even convert a few to Rational Selfishness without saying a word. Don't be disappointed if the hardcore irrationally selfish individual remains unaffected by your motivational thoughts, feelings and actions. And definitely don't allow these neurotic people to drain your energy and drag you down to their level. You possess your Dynamic Weapons and you know how to use them.

Manifesting the Dynamic Joy of Existence Weapon

You journeyed long and far. You saw through the delusions of Social Altruists, successfully confronted irrational selfishness and happily discovered Rational Selfishness. You continued on the path meeting one illusion after another. You realized that conquering life's illusions might be an never-ending battle. Fortunately, you picked up some Dynamic Weapons along the way. Most of the time your life as an impeccable warrior is fun, exciting and rewarding—but not always. Sometimes you endure moments of doubt that sabotage your feelings of happiness. You notice your pathway is littered with obstacles and blocks. Frustration sneaks into your consciousness. Eventually you pull out the appropriate Dynamic Weapons. You Ready, Aim, Fire. You were up to the challenge. However, it wasn't a pleasant or happy experience.

I remember a time of my uncertainty and frustration. I realized a professional situation had placed me in a headlock with no escape. Now that's an illusion! As I often do when confronted with problems, I drove to a scenic park with the hope that the colors and sounds of nature would sooth my soul. I walked about a mile through the woods enjoying the reds, browns and oranges of autumn. I allowed the buzz of insects to quiet my mind as a mantra quiets the mind. Finally I came upon a pond vibrant with life. I discovered a park bench, sat down and observed the ducks lazily moving across the water. In addition a couple of swans displayed their grace and beauty. The warmth of the sun and the mild breeze of fall sent me into a relaxed meditative state. Suddenly I felt euphoric and knew everything was going to be fine. I experienced the joy of my existence and manifested something wonderful and enlightening. I possessed the Dynamic Joy of Existence Weapon.

Why wait until you accomplish your DEFINITE PURPOSE or other secondary goals to experience the joy of your existence? Once you put your new Dynamic Weapon into use little things take on a new meaning. The aroma of the honeysuckle on a mild spring day, the depths of your meditations, the sublime feelings from the music you experience, the touch of your lover's hand, the thrill of integrating complex concepts, the inspiration you receive from a new idea create wondrous, enriching experiences. You completely experience reality. Doesn't that feel like something you would like to possess right now?

Here's something you'll like. Surprisingly, even your body feels different. Some mystics call sexual activities low-level experiences. Honestly, I believe practicing celibacy is a low-level way to exist. An enlightened person is sensuous and sexual. He or she experiences the pleasures of the flesh to the utmost and delights in their partners flesh to the max. In fact, the Rationally Selfish Individual transforms the sexual experience into an ecstasy of the body, mind and spirit.

Maybe you're wondering where I found the Dynamic Joy of Existence Weapon. Was it perched up against a tree or sitting on the ground near the waters edge? Richard Wagner, the great German composer, knew where to find it. He revealed *"Joy is not in things; it is in us."* Before you can capture outer joy, you must unleash your inner joy. The Dynamic Joy of Existence Weapon resides within all of us. It's up to you to find it. Your Dynamic Weapons of Mind Power and Accelerated Awareness should aid you in your search. And, of course, you are Rational Selfishness.

Protecting Your New Dynamic Weapon

As incredible as it might seem, when you express the joy of your existence you will often run head first into the negative reactions of others. Sometimes those closest to you will generate the greatest resistance. As I mentioned, it's impossible to completely avoid Social Altruists and irrationally selfish people. Many of your relatives and business acquaintances will never accept Rational Selfishness.

8 Dynamic Weapons for Conquering Life's Illusions

Fortunately, you have your Dynamic Weapons to protect you. Ready, Aim, Fire.

You must understand that your Dynamic Joy of Existence Weapon protects your from your self-defeating conscious and subconscious thoughts and feelings. It allows you to express pleasure, ecstasy and happiness. It's not the Dynamic Weapon of choice when your enemies threaten your personal liberty and economic freedom. In fact, you need your other Dynamic Weapons to protect it. Happily, it will help you attract other like-minded Rationally Selfish Individuals into your life. Nothing like having allies.

Let's say you're experiencing the pure joy that comes from listening to beautiful inspiring music, enjoying the many facets of nature, meditating or reading a book that stirs your spirit to a accelerated way of thinking and feeling. You're happily experiencing the joy of your existence—and then along comes an unhappy person who criticizes you for dancing like a fool, being a lazy loafer, thinking thoughts that are way out there or actually being way out there. In other words, he or she attempts to rain on your majestic parade. You know what to do. Instead of letting anger overcome you, you reach for your Dynamic Anti-Irrational Selfishness Weapon. Ready, Aim Fire. Repeat. You successfully protected your new weapon.

You must face the fact that repressed, neurotic people won't understand where you're coming from. Some people sink so low in their unhappiness, they hate seeing you express the pure joy of your existence or indulging in the activities that help you reach accelerated states of awareness. The irrationally selfish person mercilessly baits you into responding to his negativity. He cruelly attempts to bring you down to his low level of awareness.

When you experience the bliss that comes from the joy of your existence it's a shock to have someone attempt to knock you down. You wonder why he or she would do this to you. Your first reaction will be to defend yourself minus the use of your Dynamic Weapons. You become defensive and the next thing you know you're involved in a heated argument. Before you know what hit you, you're in the gutter of negative thoughts, abusive words and destructive actions. You allowed an irrationally selfish person to capture your Dynamic Joy of Existence

Weapon—and he or she won't even know how to use it.

I know it can happen from my own experiences. Many times I let someone bait me into reacting to their negativity. Neurotic people dumped mental and emotional garbage on me as I was experiencing the joy of my existence. It took years for me find the Dynamic Weapons that would protect me from their unwarranted attacks. Hopefully, you learn self-protection considerably faster than I did—and you should since I'm leading you to the Dynamic Weapons.

Here's what you can do to protect your Dynamic Joy of Existence Weapon using your Dynamic Anti-Irrational Selfishness Weapon. I will assume you aren't walking around naked. What's amazing is that you will effectively disarm the person attacking you.

1. Temporarily retreat from the action and make sure you have the appropriate Dynamic Weapons available for action.
2. Take several deep breaths and slowly count from 10 to 0, gradually achieving a state of calmness by releasing built up stress and negativity.
3. Confront your enemy as an impeccable warrior would confront him or her. State your case or point of view in a calm, easy manner. Accept any feedback you receive without getting defensive. You must monitor your reaction. The instinctive thing to do is to become defensive and fight back. Remember the impeccable warrior, the Rationally Selfish Individual TAKES CHARGE of his thoughts, feelings and actions. It's possible you win the battle now; however when you're dealing with an irrationally selfish person-------------.
4. If negative emotions continue to flare up walk away before your Dynamic Joy of Existence Weapon vanishes. This isn't always easy. It takes a certain amount of willpower, but you are an impeccable warrior—aren't you?
5. Return to the present moment. Center yourself in positive, creative thoughts. I have found that listening to some of my favorite music will defuse my negative emotions and replace them with joyous, positive emotions. Anyway, reach out for one of your favorite things. You just saved your Dynamic Joy of

Existence Weapon.

A Tale of Two Couples

During one particularly lovely spring day 23 years ago two young couples were preparing for their June wedding. As best friends they had double dated on many occasions and were looking forward to married life with excitement and anticipation. As with most young couples they believed "They would get married and live happily ever after."

Both couples did similar things in their married life. Both have two children. Both own their homes. Their incomes were similar for years. They enjoyed many extracurricular activities together, such as bowling in the same Thursday night league.

Now 23 years later they're experiencing the empty nest syndrome as their children are off to college. That's where the similarity ends.

One couple expresses excitement about life. They started a part-time business that is rapidly becoming successful. Their loving sex life supplies them more pleasure than when they were newlyweds. When you observe them, you see their vibrancy and feel their high energy. Their minds function at an accelerated level of awareness. They fill their married life with love, intellectual inspiration, great music and new opportunities. Here's a man and woman who captured the pleasures of the body, mind and spirit. They experience the joy of their existence.

The other couple is tired and worn out—and it shows in their faces and demeanor. They hate their jobs but don't know a way out. They have sex maybe once a month, barely enjoying it. They come home at night; eat supper, hardly tasting their food and crash in front of the TV. Sometimes they try to party, but that only results in drunkenness, verbal battles, depression and hangovers. They are confused about the meaning of life. They have no idea what it's all about. Their life is drab, unrewarding and without hope.

These two couples, who were once best friends, are growing apart. What happened? Why is the first couple living with zest and the other is barely living?

You know the answers. Once couple embraced the life of Rational

Selfishness and discovered the joy of their existence, while the other couple lacks a DEFINITE PURPOSE and sinks in the abyss of irrational selfishness.

Your life isn't meant to be polluted with emotional pain and suffering. You give it the blessings of pleasure and ecstasy. After all, you use each precious moment to create the life you desire. Your Dynamic Weapons skyrocket as invaluable gifts that protect you from Social Altruism and irrational selfishness—your own and that of neurotic people.

Inspirational Quote: *Imagine for a moment that it is possible for you to experience the joy of your existence, no matter what is happening around you.*

You get the idea. You happily embark on a journey of personal liberty and freedom that maximizes the enjoyment of your body, mind and spirit. Emotional fulfillment, mental stimulation and diverse pleasures will be daily experiences. Many of the ecstasies of life are yours for the taking. Finally you'll be free to live your DEFINITE PURPOSE and enjoy the secondary goals and desires that add spice to your life—or maybe you still have doubts about the morality of Rational Selfishness. I think it's about time to erase your doubts. Uncertainty about using your Dynamic Weapons doesn't make you a very efficient soldier of personal liberty and economic freedom. It's very difficult to conquer life's illusions if you hesitate to use them. And abandoning your Dynamic Rational Selfishness Weapon_____.

Maybe you're thinking this lifestyle isn't very spiritual or that maybe it is "gulp" selfish. Didn't we distinguish between Rational and irrational selfishness? Anyway, I guarantee that acting rationally in your own self interest and utilizing your mind and body to their fullest potential is moral and spiritual. Sacrificing your life to a faulty moral system and (or) the anti-life philosophy of Social Altruism is destructive and self defeating.

Jesus opposed Social Altruists and irrationally selfish people such as the chief priests, scribes, elders, Pharisees, and Sadducees. 2000 years ago, these violators of individual rights populated the political and religious establishment. As much as things change, they still remain the same.

They challenged Jesus' authority in Mark 11:27-28 King James Version.

27 And they come again to Jerusalem: and as he was walking in the temple, there come to him the chief priests, and the scribes, and the elders,

28 And say unto him, By what authority doest thou these things? and who gave thee this authority to do these things?

Jesus responded by what is know as the "Porcupine" close in sales. He threw it back to them.

Mark 11:29 King James Version
29 But Jesus answered and said to them "I also will ask you one question; then answer Me, and I will tell you by what authority I do these things:

I think we can conclude that Jesus was an impeccable warrior.

Your Highest Values

Experiencing the joy of your existence requires you to discover your highest values. We briefly covered the subject when we discussed your DEFINITE PURPOSE in Life. If it doesn't correspond to your highest values you need to change direction.

The Rationally Selfish Individual asks pertinent questions in his quest for personal liberty and economic freedom. Getting the most out of your Dynamic Weapons means you use the ammo of your highest values. Some of the potent ammo will be reason, logic, love, intuition, perseverance, integrity, compassion, initiative, self-control, imagination, enthusiasm, meditation, self-confidence etc. etc. In addition, some of your psychological arsenal of attack and self-defense will consist of values that are unique to you.

When you act from your highest values you enter into activities that are important to you. I hope your highest values don't involve irrationally selfish activities. In reality those eventually result in nonvalues. The Rationally Selfish Individual will not adopt what someone else thinks is pleasurable, valuable or important. He disdains second-hand values because he or she can never live a fulfilling life by accepting them.

The first thing you must ask is what activities deliver you the greatest pleasure. What do I want to indulge in? What do I fantasize about? What will permanently unleash the joy of my existence?

Let me ask you this question. What is your vision of what you can and will pursue and achieve? The following quote should stimulate your imagination

"Joy is the goal of existence, and joy is not to be stumbled upon, but to be achieved, and the act of treason is to let its vision drown in the swamp of the moment's torture." Ayn Rand, Atlas Shrugged.

The impeccable warrior, the Rationally Selfish Individual acts on his highest values. Since the joy of your existence depends on you discovering these, it's important that you complete this simple and enjoyable exercise.

Answer the following questions.

1. What type of sexual pleasures do I desire? Am I living my sexual fantasies now? Is my current relationship (if applicable) filled with loving sex?
2. What are my appetites for food and drink? What are my favorite dishes? What beverages do I enjoy? Do I eat in a healthy self-enhancing manner?
3. Am I watching movies that entertain me—or do I watch whatever is available even if it doesn't particularly please me?
4. Do I listen to my favorite music or accept what everyone else listens to? What music would stir my soul, move my emotions and supply me pure pleasure.
5. What style of clothes do I wear? Do I dress in the styles that are popular whether they make me feel good or not? It's possible that "if it's in it's out." **Recommendation:** You might want to look into John T. Molloy's book *"New* Dress for Success"
6. How about the automobile I drive? Is it me? Does it transform

my driving experience? You probably want to balance style with practicality.
7. Are my living arrangements to my satisfaction? Do I prefer a house or an apartment? Am I living in my dream home? Does my home encompass my desires and personality? Is this the area of town I want to live in?
8. Question your TV viewing habits. Are the shows I'm watching increasing my gratification or deadening my senses? Could I be doing something else that would give me greater satisfaction? Does my TV viewing interfere with my pursuit of my DEFINITE PURPOSE?
9. Is my career only something I have to do to make money in order to survive? Is there some other type of work that could be both enjoyable and financially rewarding? Are there occupations that give me the personal freedom to enjoy my favorite pastimes? Is my occupation in harmony with my sense of life? Have I discovered my DEFINITE PURPOSE?
10. Do I have hobbies that increase my enjoyment of life? What would I get a kick out of doing?
11. Do I feel intellectually and metaphysically stimulated? Am I a fully functioning individual? What must I do to have personal satisfaction? Does my sense of life help me or hinder me?
12. Ask yourself any other questions you can think of.

Write down everything that comes to mind. Don't be concerned about what others think of your desires. It's also important to eliminate any feelings of irrational guilt you might have about your highest values. Guilt will destroy any chance you have of capturing the joy of your existence. The freedom to choose whatever you desire is your perfect right. You are a unique individual who deserves to experience your life, your way. Should you discover some of your answers reek of irrational selfishness you know what to do. Pull out the appropriate Dynamic Weapons. Ready, Aim, Fire—as often as necessary. You may need your ammo of meditation to get to the root of your self-defeating desires.

Give this a considerable amount of thought. Sleep on it. There may be other questions you want to ask.

It's important you have a clear picture of your highest values. These are the goals that propel you to the life you deserve. They are the bedrock of obtaining and retaining the Dynamic Joy of Existence Weapon.

Seven Principles of the Joy of Existence for the Rationally Selfish Individual to Embrace

For you to completely experience the joy of your existence you must follow ironclad principles. You're already familiar with some of them. The Rationally Selfish Individual embraces them, the irrationally selfish person ignores them.

Realize that these are principles to help you enjoy the pleasures of life—not some false moral code others impose on you. These are principles for living as an impeccable warrior lives.

The first principle is:

Everyone acts in what they believe to be their own best interest

If you don't understand this ironclad principle you're in serious trouble. You're knee high in some deep sh_ , and your Dynamic Weapons disappeared under the manure. There are no exceptions to this rule. Self-interest means survival. Saints would feel uneasy if they couldn't be involved in activities that help people. Trading value for value benefits all who participate in the exchange. You will enjoy activities with other people who feel it's in their best interest to satisfy your desires—so you'll willingly satisfy their desires.

Social Altruists talk as if self interest is mean, selfish and despicable. Fortunately, you know they will tell any lie or half-truth to get you to submit to their anti-life philosophy of selflessness and self-sacrifice. Anybody with half-a-brain knows it's contrary to reason and rationality for you to act in ways that sabotage your self-interest. Even irrationally selfish people believe they act from self-interest. It's just that neurotic men and women unwittingly accept life's illusions. You use your Dynamic Weapons to conquer them.

When Social Altruists unreasonably demand that you practice selflessness and self-sacrifice, they really want you to sacrifice your self-interest for their self-interest. Time to put your Dynamic Anti-Social Altruism Weapon into use. Ready, Aim, Fire until you see the vermin on the run.

The second principle:

You trade value for value to receive what it is you desire

A sexual relationship provides a perfect example of a value for value exchange. Both individuals must receive maximum satisfaction to experience intense pleasure. Obtaining the heights of sexual ecstasy remains one of the great pleasures of an earthly existence—which is why some refer to it as heavenly.

When individuals exchange a good or service, both the buyer and seller believe they receive more value than they give.

You value a friendship because of the emotional satisfaction you receive. For a friendship to endure it must satisfy both parties.

A business relationship thrives because everyone involved believes they profit from their activities.

Go the extra mile and give as much value as possible. Napoleon Hill says *"Render more and better service than you are paid for, and sooner or later you will receive compound interest from your investment. It is inevitable that every seed of useful service you sow will sprout and reward you with an abundant harvest."* You will be amazed at all the good things that appear in your life. You reap what you sow.

Warning: Going the extra mile only benefits you if you're dealing with someone who trades value for value. I double dare you to try it with a Social Altruist. See how fast he can disarm you of your Dynamic Weapons.

It is in your best interest to avoid those who try to extort value from you. People with criminal minds such as Social Altruists, members of the political and financial establishment and common crooks attempt to receive value without giving any in return.

Unfortunately, it is sometimes difficult to avoid politicians because they are members of that apparatus of violent compulsion and coercion—the government. Fortunately, your Dynamic Weapons cut through their illusions. These violators of individual rights fear the Dynamic Unhampered Capitalism Weapon. If enough people adopted Rational Selfishness and properly armed themselves with this potent weapon, they would force members of the political establishment to find honest jobs.

As much as is humanly possible—attempt to deal only with individuals who trade value for value.

And remember. All of your highest values imply love—love of life—and love of the wonderful people and things that are part of your life. Love is some potent ammo. You probably noticed Cupid's arrow.

According to the Wikipedia Encyclopedia: *"In classical mythology,* **Cupid** *(Latin Cupido, meaning "desire") is the god of desire, erotic love, attraction and affection. He is often portrayed as the son of the love goddess Venus, and is known in Latin also as Amor ("Love"). His Greek counterpart is Eros."* Your Dynamic Joy of Existence Weapon loves love.

The third principle:

You attract into your life what you focus your mind on (whether you do it consciously or unconsciously)

You focus on negative results when you constantly think about what you don't want. You certainly can't expect to accomplish your DEFINITE PURPOSE and your highest values with a self-defeating mind set.

Keep your mind on what you desire. You possess the Dynamic Weapons of Mind Power and Accelerated Awareness to keep your attention focused on positive thoughts and results. When you include visualization and affirmations in some of your meditations, you program your mind for success.

One reason I had you make a list of your values and desires is so you would start focusing your mind on them. A focused mind is a productive mind.

Irrationally selfish people allow their minds to atrophy. These second-handers usually accept whatever the establishment media spoon feeds them. The brainwashing goes on and on ad nauseum. Makes you wonder how anyone could live with a polluted mind. Social Altruists, politicians, and news media pundits have a field day with the propaganda they espouse. Is it any wonder why the vast majority of people's "ideas" about economics and politics reside in an haze of ignorance? Sometimes, a few of these confused men and women rebel, but it's in a self-destructive way. Demonstrating your displeasure with violent social acts or self-immolation takes irrational selfishness into the absurd. An independent thinker has an integrated mind—free of illusions and myths.

When it comes to your deepest desires—passion prevails as the emotion that has the greatest power to attract them. Erase all doubts and fears. Focus your heat of passion on what you desire. You will receive it. Load the your Dynamic Joy of Existence Weapon with the ammo of passion. Ready, Aim, Fire. Your journey of DEFINITE PURPOSE zooms to the stratosphere.

The fourth principle:

Every activity involves time

Everything takes a certain amount of time. Time is an "a priori" category of human action. An "a priori" is an ultimate given. It's not possible for you to imagine non-time.

Time is a limited resource. You have only so many hours in a day to accomplish your goals and desires. Irrationally selfish people waste precious time. The Rationally Selfish Individual makes every effort to insure that each minute counts.

Decide what your values in life are—and devote you time and effort to manifesting them. If you desire a loving relationship, fine wine, beautiful music, intellectual stimulation, a rewarding occupation, a luxury sedan, a 2 story 5 bedroom house near a wooded area do what it takes to get them. Concentrate all your effort on receiving your highest values.

If circumstances or your own unwise choices have you bogged down in unrewarding activities, you must prepare to nip them in the bud. You may experience some short-term pain and discomfort, but what you gain far exceeds the price of change.

Another possible scenario is that you have allowed your comfort zone to imprison you. Remember the story in Chapter 6 under the subtitle of "Let's Rock the Boat." It's actually possible for a person to find comfort in his cell of illusion. When a Rationally Selfish Individual suddenly adopts a complacent attitude that seems to be growing on him, he reaches for his Dynamic Accelerated Awareness Weapon. He knows immediate action provides the cure. Ready, Aim, Fire. He finishes off the mortal enemy of complacency with his Dynamic Mind Power Weapon.

Benjamin Franklin said *'You may delay, but time will not."* He also stated *"Lost Time is never found again."*

The fifth principle:

You acknowledge the Law of Diminishing Returns

Economists refer to the Law of Diminishing Returns as the Marginal Theory of Value. If you don't pay heed to this law, you seriously reduce your efficiency and your pleasures. This law ties in with the principle of time. The Rationally Selfish Individual acknowledges the Law of Diminishing Returns.

There are only so many activities you can indulge in during your waking hours. If you overdo one pleasure it's at the expense of another. Also too much of a good thing quickly becomes a negative. The Law of Diminishing Returns guarantees that a person who suffers from an addiction slides down the road to hell—that is if he hasn't already arrived. An addicted person believes he has to keep increasing the activity in question to receive the same result—which obviously can't happen. He will never capture the desired outcome.

Let's say you are sipping fine wine or your favorite spirits and enjoying your favorite music. As your consumption of alcohol increases you become more receptive to the music. You unleash inner emotional feelings which increases your sensitivity to the music.

You finally reach the point where you feel absolutely great and the music provides you pure pleasure. We call that a peak experience.

Unfortunately your peak experience has limited duration. Another drink cuts your sublime experience short. In fact, it dulls your senses. You've reached the point where another drink and a favorite song gives you less satisfaction and maybe none at all. The music goes right by you. You might even conk out from the drinking.

Of course when you pass this point you aren't fit to indulge in any other favorite activities. Your over-consumption of alcohol diminishes your intellectual abilities. For a man, loving sex is probably out of the question.

The same with overindulgence in food. There may be times when your only desire is to make a glutton out of yourself. However, if you're constantly too sluggish from feeling like a stuffed turkey—then it's at the expense of the joy of your existence.

Any activity can reach the point of diminishing returns. For people with compulsive personalities this can be difficult to accept. Regardless, it's a fact of life. Your best Dynamic Weapon to combat the tendency to race past the point of no return is Rational Selfishness. You efficiently wield the Dynamic Weapon and you exist as the Dynamic Weapon. If you forget it, I'm going to bop you one. Well, not really, but I'm sure you get the point.

The sixth principle:

Balance in life maximizes the joy of your existence

This principle ties in with the Law of Diminishing Returns. In fact all the principles interconnect rather nicely.

If you want to experience the joy of your existence you must make time for the activities you enjoy. Overindulgence in one activity takes time away from another.

You want to eat food that gives you maximum satisfaction. You desire loving sex. You would like time to listen to your favorite music. There are movies and television shows you want to watch. You need intellectual stimulation to keep your mind sharp. You definitely require time to work on your DEFINITE PURPOSE.

Of course, there are chores that won't contribute much to your enjoyment of life, although there are ways of turning these into satisfying experiences. For example, getting the laundry done, loading the dishes into the dishwasher, taking out the garbage, vacuuming the carpet, washing the car, etc. Personal grooming also takes up time. It's possible to feel out of balance. You feel like you need to get everything done, but the stress of it all actually reduces your efficiency. You've lost control of your time. You're completely unbalanced

How do you restore balance to your life. The Rationally Selfish Individual TAKES CHARGE of his thoughts feelings and actions. He will pull out his Dynamic Weapons of Mind Power and Accelerated Awareness, load them with the ammo of meditation—and once again find his Dynamic Joy of Awareness Weapon.

The irrationally selfish person compounds the above by wasting precious time. He (she) destroys the chance to live a happy, productive life.

What can you do to avoid the time wasting trap? Write your goals daily. List what activities you want to indulge in. Then make sure you do them. Do not sacrifice higher values for lower values. Ask "What is the best use of my time now? Am I currently experiencing the joy my existence?"

The seventh principle:

There's no such thing as a free lunch

It's human nature to desire something for nothing. You know there's no such thing as a free lunch. Irrationally selfish people feast at the Social Altruists unhealthy banquet table of free goodies—oblivious of the discomforting "indigestion" they will soon suffer. Reality tells you the piper always demands payment plus compound interest when you buy into an illusion. You use your Dynamic Weapons to conquer life's illusions.

You can't reasonably expect something for nothing. You have to give to receive. In many cases other people will supply you the means to enjoy the good things in life. What are you offering them in return?

If you're a man and want to receive the best a woman has to offer—take her on the magic carpet of sexual ecstasy. And try to be understanding of her various moods and rich emotions. She probably has a fascinating inner life—which you may want to discover.

If a woman desires to feel sexy for her partner she may wear inviting lingerie and an erotic fragrance. Her enticing appearance and delectable scent could possibly move her partner to a high state of arousal—and increase the sexual satisfaction she experiences.

If you desire to live in a free society where people value personal liberty and economic freedom, it is critical that you understand the laws of human action and support unhampered capitalism. Social Altruists use the unsavory uneconomic systems of socialism and government interventionism to hoodwink irrationally selfish people into believing free lunches are not only possible—but for the good of "society." Time to access your arsenal of Dynamic Weapons. Your Dynamic Unhampered Capitalism Weapon blows away economic ignorance and scatters Social Altruists in all directions. Economic enlightenment begins eliminating the poverty and human misery that Social Altruists feed on.

Once again the seven principles are:

1. Everyone acts in what they believe to be their own best interest.
2. You trade value for value to receive what it is you desire.
3. You attract into your life what you focus your mind on (whether you do it consciously or unconsciously).
4. Every activity involves time.
5. You acknowledge the Law of Diminishing Returns.
6. Balance in life maximizes the joy of your existence.
7. There's no such thing as a free lunch.

As you can see—these principles refute ludicrous ideas—such as the "virtues" of selflessness, self-sacrifice and altruism. The Rationally Selfish Individual embraces and internalizes them.

Irrationally selfish people avoid the seven principles as if they were the plague. Social Altruists pretend they don't exist. These purveyors of human misery prefer to destroy all that is sublime with their anti-life illogic, unreason and nonsense. Let's get out our Dynamic Weapons and start blasting away.

The philosophy of Rational Selfishness is the only one that corresponds to the nature of man.

The anti-life philosophy of Social Altruism has failed miserably in practice. Why has it fell flat on its face? Because it advocates selflessness and self-sacrifice. It maliciously denies the sanctity of the individual. It is antagonistic to rational self-interest. It poisons and slowly destroys any society that attempts to practice it, just as it is destroying the American Way of Life. It is the philosophy of anti-life—the way of the savage.

Here's the bottom line. The anti-life philosophy of Social Altruism causes massive violations of individual rights. Social Altruists viciously attack your personal liberty and economic freedom. Continue to reload your Dynamic Anti-Social Altruism Weapon and fire away.

Irrationally selfish people cannot continue to live at the expense of others and expect to reap a bountiful crop of prosperity and abundance. Once the virtues of self-reliance, honesty and productive effort vanish, all that is good and sublime fades away. The Rationally Selfish Individual relishes truth and justice—and he will protect them with every Dynamic Weapon he possesses. Why wouldn't he? They rate among his highest values. In addition, truth and justice sits proudly with his other ammo.

Conclusion

You captured another Dynamic Weapon. That makes 7 of them in your psychological arsenal of attack and self defense.

1. Anti-Social Altruism
2. Anti-Irrational Selfishness
3. Rational Selfishness
4. Unhampered Capitalism
5. Mind Power
6. Accelerated Awareness
7. Joy of Existence

We continue to move on with purpose. It's time to capture another Dynamic Weapon.

Every action you take, every feeling you feel, in fact, every outcome you experience, inside and out, is the result of a strategy. All day long, you unconsciously run through a constant stream of strategies. - Bill Harris

CHAPTER NINE

DYNAMIC STRATEGIC ACTION WEAPON

You possess an impressive psychological arsenal of Dynamic Weapons. You know what your DEFINITE PURPOSE in Life is. You recognize your external and internal enemies. You have taken charge of your thoughts and feelings. Unfortunately when the time for battle arrives you're unable to pull the trigger. You lack the action habit. You might as well walk around naked and unarmed for all the good your Dynamic Weapons are doing you.

The Rationally Selfish Individual realizes he must take action in order to satisfy his goals and desires. *"An ant on the move does more than a dozing ox."* - Lao Tzu. If you sit on your butt wishin' and a hopin', irrationally selfish people might pass you up. It's obvious that success and fulfillment requires the impetuous of action.

When Mises wrote "Human Action" he didn't title it "Human Procrastination." The heroes in Rand's "Atlas Shrugged" refused to allow Social Altruists to continue victimizing them. These Rationally Selfish Individuals took the action of withdrawing all support of a parasitical society to expedite its collapse. Now that's using the Dynamic Weapons with deadly precision. All success—without exception—is the result of action.

Maybe your goals excite you, but the actions you must take to achieve them seem rather unpleasant. Thomas Edison said *"The successful person has the habit of doing the things failures don't like to do."* In Chapter Eight, I reminded you "there's no such thing as a free lunch." You must pay the price for success. Let's acquire your new Dynamic Weapon.

Your Dynamic Weapon of Strategic Action conquers procrastination. In addition it insures you take productive actions that create the success you desire. Without a well-defined strategy, it's difficult to arrive at your destination. How will you accomplish your DEFINITE PURPOSE without a purposeful plan? If you make very little progress because you bounce here, there, everywhere and even nowhere, your frustration could allow procrastination to wrestle control from you. You know that's completely unacceptable. The impeccable warrior, the Rationally Selfish Individual TAKES CHARGE of his thoughts, feelings and actions.

The Strategic Advantage

Bill Harris creator of the highly recommended "Life Integration Principles" course says. *"Every action you take, every feeling you feel, in fact, every outcome you experience, inside and out, is the result of a strategy. All day long, you unconsciously run through a constant stream of strategies. You have strategies for love, hate, learning, forgetting, parenting, sports, communicating, selling, buying, motivation, sex, health, disease, creativity, relaxation, fun, boredom, anxiety, depression, poverty, wealth— and for everything else."*

The Rationally Selfish Individual prefers to create his strategies, although having successful ones run on automatic gives him an advantage. There's only so much time in a day. Running around aimlessly because you're bullied by unconscious strategies doesn't lead you to the path of success and happiness. Unfortunately, the irrationally selfish person does just that. Soon it's Social Altruists to the "rescue." Can you imagine dealing with one of those parasites naked and unarmed. That's what you call a nightmare. Neurotics are so far gone that they consider a Social Altruist "A Knight in Shining Armor." You know you've hit the skids when you're reduced to a helpless man or woman who needs protection from reality.

What you want to do is analyze each area of your life where you're not achieving the results you desire. Chances are your strategy just doesn't cut the mustard. You've fallen for some of life's illusions. Now here's where want to access your arsenal of Dynamic Weapons. Arm yourself with your Dynamic Weapons of Mind Power and Accelerated Awareness and load it with the ammo of meditation. Your secondary ammo consists of reason and intuition. Once you come up with a new strategy you pull out your Dynamic Strategic Action Weapon and get moving. I guess it's obvious your new Dynamic Weapon requires the ammo of action and more action. It's similar to a Burst Mode Firearm, like the AN-94, that has a "hyperburst," a feature in which rounds are fired in incredibly quick succession (1800 rpm in the case of the AN-94). Since money and success loves speed, you now possess a strategic advantage.

Procrastination has more lives than the proverbial cat. In fact, I'm convinced it's immortal, which means it's a never ending battle to defeat it. Whatever you do don't misplace you're new Dynamic Weapon. There are some days you'll have to force yourself to use it. Here's quote for you. It's been stated in many different ways so I'm taking liberties with it. *"Procrastination knocked on the door. Passion, desire and strategic action answered. No one was there."*

When is the time to take action? Well it isn't tomorrow or next week or next month. It isn't when you finally have a perfect plan. It isn't when you feel better. It isn't when your problems are solved. It is now! And I mean now! The Rationally Selfish Individual acts as an impeccable warrior acts.

Another Wasted Day

Well, it's another day. I wish I felt like doing something. I don't have a job to go to. I might as well go back to sleep. Damn, thinking wakes me up. What a curse. I guess, I'll have to drag my carcass out of bed. I wish I didn't have morning breathe. Now I have to brush my teeth. I better first make coffee. Otherwise, there's no hope for doing anything. Why does life have to be so hard?

It seems like once I graduated from high school nothing was ever the same. Come to think of it that wasn't always so great. I barely made it. At least there were girlfriends, some drug parties and few beer bashes. I enjoyed speeding up and down Highway 323 in the souped up 1997 Dodge Viper GTS my dad bought me. That was a stretch of about 13 miles. I must have done it thousands of times. I always ended where I started. My life's like that, only I teeter back and forth in a slow rut. I wish my dad could help me out but he disowned me. He called me a worthless, lazy bum. That's no way to treat a son.

I could watch some morning TV, but all that celebrity BS makes me feel worse. Some people have all the luck. Maybe I should play a video game. Only problem with that is unless I put my brain to work I have to use the cheat codes to make any progress. Ah, I don't feel like doing that. You know I could access some porn on the internet. The trouble with that is it makes me horny—and self-stimulation doesn't do a thing for me. I wish I had a girlfriend. I thought my last relationship would last. One day she started making up excuses why she wouldn't go out with me. Finally she wouldn't take my calls or respond to my text messages. I don't have any motivation to find another one. Anyway, who would want me. I don't even like myself very much. The world has always been out to get me and it's beaten me down. Sometimes I wonder if there's something wrong with me. Otherwise, I wouldn't take people's crap.

It seems like nothing inspires me. I use to enjoy my favorite music. Now it goes right by me. I must admit, I feel emotionally dead. I could go to the doctor and get a prescription for anti-depressants but I don't have any extra money or health insurance. I wonder if I'm eligible for free ObamaCare.

All that's left is for me is to get in my easy chair and turn on the TV. If the programs bore me I can always doze off. I have a frozen pizza I can put in the oven when I get hungry. That means I have to get up and turn on the stove. Oh well, you've gotta eat. Why do I feel like this is just another wasted day?

It appears his subconscious strategies of failure, frustration and unhappiness run on automatic. Tragically, every facet of his life relies on the same self-defeating strategies. He oblivious to the fact that he must TAKE CHARGE of his thoughts, feelings and actions. He's hopelessly sitting around naked with absolutely no Dynamic Weapons.

Maybe it's unfair that his dad called him a worthless, lazy bum and cut him off. It's possible the "old man" spoiled him rotten and never taught him the virtue of self-reliance. Regardless, reality doesn't care one way or another. It deals out results according to cause and effect relationships—some which it hides from us mere mortals. That's one reason conquering life's illusion requires a lifetime purposeful effort. When the Grim Reaper arrives you can only hope your Dynamic Weapons go with you—or maybe where you're going you won't need them. Is death good or bad? According to the Wikipedia Encyclopedia *"In Poland, Death,or Śmierć, has an appearance similar to the traditional*

Grim Reaper, but instead of a black robe, Death has a white robe."

Back to what we're dealing with—and that's life—precious life. Aren't you glad you're the Dynamic Rational Selfishness Weapon?

Increase the Efficiency of Your Dynamic Weapons by Exercising

You knew it was coming. You are going to have to do several things to maximize your employment of your Dynamic Weapons. You know by know "There's no such thing as a free lunch." I'm going to mention that "dirty" word exercise. It's time to put your Dynamic Strategic Action Weapon into action in order to force yourself to do it. Maybe you've heard someone talk about the thrill of exercise. Well, I admit that I've never found it to be thrilling. I have to force myself to firm up my body. I'm not perfect. I still struggle with my weight—but at least I feel good and have developed some muscle. If I didn't work out I would have a real problem with excess weight.

When most people attempt an exercise program they fail and give up after several weeks. There are several reasons for this.

One reason is—it's hard to remain dedicated to an unpleasant task when you don't see immediate results.

Another reason is that exercise is time consuming. You probably believe you are required to enroll in a health club, use precious time and go there at least 3 days a week. Plus health clubs cost money.

I am expelling the above myths. You don't have to kill yourself with mega-exercise programs or spend a lot of money to get into shape.

Of course if that's what you like doing, go for it. If not, I will show you how easy it is to get the required exercise that enhances the joy of your existence. You just discovered some ammo for one of your Dynamic Weapons. Your Dynamic Rational Selfishness Weapon also likes it.

Note: Consult a physician before beginning any exercise program.

My first recommendation is the Metabolic Aftershock Workout. I quickly lost 2 inches off my waist. According to their website https://www.metabolicaftershock.com/ "Everything you've been told about burning fat with exercise is flat out wrong. Metabolic Aftershock introduces you to "intelligent" exercises that are short, fun, thrilling, and can be done anywhere without weights or gym equipment. These scientifically-based 45-second movements take only 15 minutes, 3 times per week, and will reprogram, recharge, and reboot your metabolism." I agree with that statement—except the "fun and thrilling" part. Of course, you must pay a price to increase the fun and thrills you will receive the rest of the day.

My next recommendation is the "Weight Destroyer Program" created by Michael Wren. What's nice is that it supplies you a full list of foods you can eat for weight control. You also receive the benefit of their 10 Minute Transformation exercise program. His website http://weight-destroyer.com/ states "This Fat-Destroying program doesn't require any prescription drugs, restrictive diets, overpriced and ineffective weight-loss products, or even calorie counting for that matter!" If you have knee problems this one is a little easier on them than the first one I recommended.

Men'sHealth recommends another exercise program called "The 10-Minute Transformation", not to be confused with the previous recommendation, even though the names for the two are similar. Visit http://www.menshealth.com/fitness/10-minute-transformation to find out about it.

In addition, walking always makes an excellent way to stay physically fit. Plus, you get to enjoy nature when you walk around your neighborhood, visit a the park, trek around a lake or hike in the woods. That's one "exercise" I enjoy. Pull out your Dynamic Strategic Action Weapon and get moving. Remember, nothing happens until something moves.

Blast Away the Brainwashing of the Social Altruist with Continuous Learning

All your Dynamic Weapons pack a powerful punch when they're loaded with the ammo of continuous learning. It's time to blast away the brainwashing of the Social Altruist by attacking his system of "education." Our strategy requires that we shoot holes through it. Let's begin.

A person leaves school and vows he will never be subject to that torture again. The result: The disillusioned individual often drifts through life with a closed mind—and a resistance to new ideas and new ways of living. Irrational selfishness seeps in and takes over his life. Eventually, he (she) settles into a comfort zone of boredom and stagnation. Finally, his life becomes unsettled, filled with one crisis after another. A changing world won't let him cling to his uninspiring routines. Eventually Social Altruists come to the "rescue." If we witness the event, we know what to do. Ready, Aim, Fire. One mission takes out two enemies.

Unfortunately, our public school system fails to instill a sense of joyous learning into young students. That's fits in with a Social Altruist's evil strategy. Kill the joy of existence before it has a chance to blossom. When precious minds are at the age when they're receptive to the ideas and wonders of the world—uninspired teachers with worn out lessons destroy their desire to learn.

I am not attempting to disparage all teachers or the profession of teaching. I was blessed with some teachers who were dedicated and highly competent. I still have fond memories of them and give them my thanks. Thanks Mrs. Reynolds, Mr. Kelso, Mrs. Earl, Miss Smith, Mr. Kaffenberg. I am sure there were others who helped me in my development.

Even worse, an establishment education gives the hapless child a set of rules and regulations to follow, routines and customs without rhyme or reason. Creativity flees from the classroom and tragically, the child's impressionable mind. The Social Altruist makes sure the child "grows" into an adult who becomes an automatic response mechanism of political correctness. It's enough to make you want to hunt down the varmints. Remember the Rationally Selfish Individual TAKES CHARGE of his thoughts, feelings and actions. He doesn't allow anyone to cause him to lose his cool.

Directives such as stay in line, color within the lines, become good little boys and girls and don't rock the boat eradicate individualistic tendencies. The child learns Rational Selfishness will not be tolerated—and that pleasing others instead of satisfying his own interests, guarantees that he will get along with the crowd, blending in with its stifling conformity. Later, peer pressure encourages more acquiescence to the group's wishes and desires—as if a group is an entity unto itself.

The impeccable warrior reports the following tale from a day in school. A friend of his received a note from his son's teacher complaining what a bad boy little Joey had been. He committed a horrible crime against conformity. When the children in line were walking to who knows where, a chair happened to appear in the way. All the kids walked to the right of the chair. However, this "rebellious" kid walked around the left side. The authoritarian teacher reprimanded him and gave him a demerit. Talk about squelching individualism.

Soon, the big day arrives when the child becomes an adult. Unfortunately, the damage is done. Irrational selfishness or even worse Social Altruism becomes a way of life. Few can escape the ravages of an establishment education. In fact, most don't realize there's an escape route from the indoctrination, the key that unlocks the cell door revealing the path to reason and independent thought. Sadly, the brainwashing has been complete and devilishly effective.

Logic tells you a person should rebel against what the establishment has done to his intellect and psyche. Instead, many revolt against knowledge, truth and justice, failing to blame the institutions that stole their mind and spirit. Most have memories of the painful hours they spent in classrooms, tortured to death by uninspired teachers. Who wants to be subject to that again.

The warrior understands how it felt to be bored to tears and to eventually rebel against the establishment's indoctrination. He skipped school anytime he could. When he showed up, he considered it "the hole" and the ride home on the bus "parole."

The above facts are pathetic. Social Altruism stifles young minds, possibly causing permanent damage. Fortunately, there is always hope. Learning is not boredom and torture. It takes you on a trip of excitement, adventure and new discoveries.

If you have been on the path of continuous learning, you're reaping great benefits. If not, I have some exciting news for you. You can begin your journey—today. And guess what? You choose what you want to read and investigate. You discover what makes you feel passionate and alive. You decide what your curriculum will be. I've quoted some authors in this book. I highly recommend them.

You kiss the illusionary establishment 'teachings' goodbye—forever. You release your mind and spirit from its imaginary grip. You begin a journey of discovery and new wonders. And you possess the Dynamic Weapons to free your mind from life's illusions and the politically correct crap Social Altruists use to enslave people. Ready, Aim, Fire and Repeat. You don't allow anyone to get in your way. For quick results access your "hyperburst" Dynamic Strategic Action Weapon.

Plan to Achieve Your Definite Purpose

Get out your Dynamic Strategic Action Weapon now. You must develop plans to achieve your DEFINITE PURPOSE in Life. Ready, Aim, Fire. As the Dynamic Weapon implies, you create an effective strategy for success and take purposeful action.

Make a list of everything you want to achieve. You will continually add to it and subtract from it. I have mine in a word doc. titled "Action." Now rate the importance of each one by placing an A, B, C, D next to it. Please don't list any F activities unless you want to remind yourself of some foolish behavior from the past to discourage you from indulging in irrationally selfish behavior. An A activity rates higher than a B activity.

How would you rate activities that correspond to your DEFINITE PURPOSE? The Rationally Selfish Individual gives those an A. Although there's nothing wrong with these shows, what letter would you place next to watching reruns of Cheers, Gilligan's Island, The Beverly Hillbillies, The Munsters or The Addams Family. The irrationally selfish man or woman probably acts as if these shows rate an A or B on the list of today's activities. I will state that if you've accomplished your A and B activities and want to relax with some comedy shows, watch them if they please you. Laughter nourishes the soul. If you work hard on your DEFINITE PURPOSE you succeed. If you overwork, you reach the Point of Diminishing Returns. The Rationally Selfish Individual enjoys the pleasures of the body, mind and spirit. I definitely take time to enjoy my favorite music and engage in activities with my girlfriend.

My list includes everything I must do to achieve my DEFINITE

PURPOSE, my financial goals, mundane things that can't wait any longer and the pleasures of the body, mind and spirit I want to indulge in.

Four important activities:

1. List everything you must do to accomplish your DEFINITE PURPOSE.
2. Write down any activities you haven't yet experienced but would like to engage in.
3. Write down anything you have previously indulged in and enjoyed, but aren't currently doing.
4. List all the obstacles and blocks that are preventing you from taking action on your goals and desires.

If you're not accomplishing your goals and desires, you need to ask yourself why. What is holding me back? Why am I unable to take action on my important values? Am I allowing others to control my life? As soon as you come up with the answers, arm yourself with the necessary Dynamic Weapons and begin firing away. The Rationally Selfish Individual conquers life's illusions.

Plain and simple. You are a unique individual. You deserve to capture the personal liberty and economic freedom that comes with the Rationally Selfish Way of Life.

Eliminate Negativity: Program Your Subconscious Mind with Success Strategies

Once again we turn to Bill Harris of Centerpointe Research Institute. *"If you are having trouble in relationships, and become attracted to people who treat you poorly, look at your attraction strategy, and change it to one that works better. If you're having trouble making money, you might want to do something about your strategy for making money, or for recognizing a potentially good money-making situation. If you have trouble learning, you might want to discover what your learning strategy is and improve it. If you have a way of becoming confused when you try to do or learn something, or become overwhelmed, there is a strategy involved, and you can change it. Becoming anxious is a strategy, and so is getting angry, getting depressed, and so on."*

Recommendation: Visit www.centerpointe.com and discover the marvelous resources he offers you for self-development.

The Rationally Selfish Individual dedicates his efforts to changing his unproductive and self-defeating strategies. He resorts to his Dynamic Weapons of Mind Power and Accelerated Awareness, first loading them with the ammo of meditation and then reason and intuition when necessary.

One method for changing undesirable subconscious strategies is affirmations. Here are ten effective affirmations for the impeccable warrior.

1. I act from Rational Selfishness. I eliminate irrationally selfish behavior from my life.
2. I think, feel and act as an impeccable warrior thinks, feels and acts.
3. I TAKE CHARGE of my thoughts, feeling and actions.
4. I take action now!
5. I never allow anyone to cause me to lose my cool. I remain calm and cool always.
6. I allow myself to possess impeccable integrity.
7. I always allow myself to live by my values and beliefs without compromise.
8. I allow myself to live from the outcome of my goals and desires.
   Note: See yourself in possession of that which you desire.
9. When in doubt, I remember that I possess a psychological arsenal of Dynamic Weapons that conquer life's illusions
10. I exist as the Dynamic Rational Selfishness Weapon.

Think about your DEFINITE PURPOSE in Life, your secondary goals and desires and create affirmations that will help you succeed.

Releasing negativity from your being helps you accomplish your goals and desires. You can't hold in negativity and expect to feel peaceful and easy. Negative thoughts and feelings sabotage your ability to achieve your DEFINITE PURPOSE and they destroy peace of mind. I understand that unwanted thoughts suddenly pop into your mind, especially when negative circumstances confront you. Here's how you handle them.

One technique, we call cleaning. Just as you clean out your closet, you clean out negative thoughts and feelings. Here's how simple it is. Now the following may sound silly, but it works.

Imagine a white light surrounding your being. Now visualize it spinning counterclockwise dissolving the blocks and obstacles it pulls from your body. You can see these blocks and obstacles as little gray balls or blocks the color of black. Also, notice the white light growing brighter and brighter during the cleaning process. When you finish the cleaning, spin the light clockwise to re-energize you.

Use the above method as often as needed.

Of course, if you believe the above is mystical nonsense, you can meditate on axiomatic concepts such as existence, identity and consciousness while releasing negative thoughts and feelings.

Exploring Self-Hypnosis

You've heard of hypnosis. Let's explore self-hypnosis. For more information visit: http://stevegjones.com/. That's how I discovered it.

You will create a wave file with your own voice that you can listen to on your computer. You may want to burn it to a CD. In order to create a Hypnotic CD you need microphone headphones for your computer. In addition you need an audio editor and recorder. You can download Audacity for free by visiting http://audacityteam.org .

You will want to include a relaxing technique, your DEFINITE PURPOSE and affirmations concerning your goals and desires.

Once again you will access your Dynamic Weapons of Mind Power and Accelerated Awareness and pack them with the ammo of meditation. Dr. Steven J Jones taught me how to create a hypnotic program and he will teach you—if you allow him. The Rationally Selfish Individual embraces continuous learning. The irrationally selfish person acts as if he already knows it all. He's so far behind in the race for success that he thinks he's in the lead. What an illusion!

Here's a sample of what I include on my hypnotic program. If you want to become an expert at something you must study it. I already made one recommendation for accelerating your self-hypnosis skills. That gives you a chance to put your Dynamic Accelerated Awareness Weapon into use. Ready, Aim, Fire.

All right, I want you to take a deep breath in through your nose, inhaling very slowly, filling your lungs and stretching them out. Hold it in to the count of 3. Open your mouth slightly and exhale very slowly, and as you do, just feel your body relaxing, relaxing, relaxing.

Take another a deep breath in through your nose, inhaling very slowly, filling your lungs and stretching them out. Hold it in to the count of 3. Open your mouth slightly and exhale very slowly, and as you do, just feel your body relaxing and relaxing more and more.

Once again, take another a deep breath in through your nose, inhaling very slowly, filling your lungs and stretching them out. Hold it in to the count of 3. Open your mouth slightly and exhale very slowly, and as you do, just feel your body relaxing more and more.

Take one more deep breath in through your nose, inhaling very slowly, filling your lungs and stretching them out. Hold it in to the count of 3. Open your mouth slightly and exhale very slowly, and as you do, just feel your body becoming completely relaxed.

Note: Talk slow and hesitate between scenes for better visualization.

Now to help you to relax, I want you to visualize that you have just entered the magical path to Grapevine Lake—the pathway of success and prosperity. It is your path, your lake and your woods. You are relaxed and safe. You easily walk along the path even though it offers obstacles and challenges in the way of rocky hills and curving walkways. You are confident you will succeed. Peace flows through your whole being. You look to your left and see the glistening lake sparkle from the rays of the sun. Now feel the glow of the sun relaxing every part of your body as it caresses you. Lift your face up and feel the comforting warmth of the sun's rays. Allow the relaxing breeze from the lake to blow gently across your body. As you walk slowly down the path, you feel the breeze ruffle your hair. Stop for a moment and breathe in the fresh air, allowing it to mellow your body and mind. You look to your right and see a wooded area. You can hear the birds chirping and singing their songs of wonder. You catch a glimpse of a redbird and now you see a blue jay. You feel and hear a branch crunch softly under your feet. The soft breeze causes the leaves to ruffle, further relaxing you. Looking up at the surrounding area you notice the clear blue sky, along with some puffy white clouds peacefully floating by. You also become aware of the different shades of green that nature displays for your pleasure.

Looking out over the lake you notice a flock of seagulls happily flying off in the distance. As you inhale the mild air, you can taste its freshness. It's like sipping a cool glass of water. You look up at the sky and notice how bright blue it is. There are several large clouds in the sky. They are big and white. You notice them moving slowly across the sky over the lake. You almost wish you could float up and relax on one.

In the distance you see several boats. Happy men and women enjoy the sun and the water. Ah, there's a young boy, his fishing pole and his expectation of a catch. He sits peacefully on the edge of the lake, patient and unaware of time. In addition, on a rock of love you catch two lovers embracing as one. Love is in the air on this marvelous spring day.

This is the season of your flowering. Before entering the woods, you come to an opening, a field of flowers displaying their rainbow colors. You see the red, orange, gold, yellow, violet and blue of spring. You smell the fragrance of the flowers. You see the bees happily gathering honey. Butterflies of every color move from flower to flower. You rest for a moment, becoming the vibration and harmony of spring.

You move on and enter the woods. Suddenly the atmosphere feels dark and foreboding. For a moment you feel uneasy, but you know you are up to the challenge because you have successfully handled each crisis that life has dealt you. Yes, you are definitely up to the challenge. You have the capacity to act effectively. You possess personal power.

You weave your way over the path listening to the many sounds of insects and other creatures of the woods. You catch a glimpse of a small animal moving quickly between the trees. Finally you come to a trail that leads to the lake. You confidently walk down the trail until you come to an inviting large rock ledge that sits comfortably above the lake.

You climb on the rock and gaze over the lake. The sun warming your body causes you to relax as one with the lake. How pleasurable it is to breathe in the freshness of the lake. The mild breeze sends you into peaceful state of being. As you lay back, you focus on relaxing your entire body. You start with your head by relaxing the muscles in your face and in your jaw. Moving down to your neck and shoulders, you relax every muscle. Feel all tension release. Your arms, hands, and fingers lay loosely by your side as you relax on the peaceful rock. Focus on relaxing your lower back, sides, and abs.

Now moving further down your body, to your hips and buttocks, you relax these muscles even more. You feel more and more relaxed. Relax your thighs. Relax your knees. Relax your calves and shins. Your legs are now completely weightless. Move down to your ankles, feet, and toes. Release all tension from your feet. Your entire body is now very relaxed. Enjoy this relaxation. Now focus on relaxing your mind. Your brain is free from random thoughts. You focus on relaxing, further melting into the soft but firm rock. You enjoy this feeling of total relaxation of your body and mind.

You lose track of time as you become one with the lake. You notice the sun is beginning to set and it will soon be dark. You feel secure because you see an easy, lighted path that leads safely back to your car. Security results from successfully overcoming challenges and achieving your goals and desires.

There you have it. Now you slowly count from 10 to 0 as you watch the sun set. It's has completely set when you reach 0. It's up to you to create affirmations for your program. In addition, you want include your DEFINITE PURPOSE. Here are some sample affirmations.

1. I overcome interruptions in my forward progress in order to benefit from the power of momentum.
2. I generate unstoppable momentum. I am unstoppable. I am unstoppable. I am unstoppable.
3. I overcome procrastination in order to achieve my goals and desires.
4. I achieve supreme physical fitness.
5. As my fat melts away my energy increases. I possess enough energy to achieve my goals and desires. I feel great.
6. I take action. I take action on my goals and desires. I accomplish

my goals and desires I possess personal power.
7. I effectively wield my Dynamic Weapons.

You can include the ten affirmations I supplied you on page 183. Use your imagination and create ones that correspond to your highest values. Here's a sample of how to include your DEFINITE PURPOSE.

This year, the year 20-- is my year of flowering. I begin earning at least $----- per month—now, increasing it each month until I reach my monthly income goal of $---- by --------- of this (next) year. That will take my income up to $---K per year. My annual income goals for the following years are: (20-- $---K) (20-- $---K) (20-- $---K) (20-- $---K) (20-- $---K) (20-- $---).

In order to reach my major DEFINITE PURPOSE, I become a (DEFINITE PURPOSE). I allow ---------------- (What are you producing or creating with your DEFINITE PURPOSE?) to open the door to my success. I form alliances that help me expand my horizons.

My DEFINITE PURPOSE is to bring to the attention of the world the possibilities of ----------------------(What are you offering?).

Note: You can substitute the word (You for I) in your hypnotic program if you believe that will be more effective. Some people respond to the 3rd party technique.

Follow this up with more affirmations. I recommend repeating each one at least 3 times, sprinkled throughout the program. You begin finishing off the hypnotic program by tricking your conscious mind into forgetting the session. You suggest that it's just too hard to remember what was said. Then you end it by counting from 1 to 4. Your hypnotic program should be 20 to 30 minutes long. When you listen to it, put on your best headphones.

The Rationally Selfish Selfish Individual likes effective procedures, so he investigates the correct methods to accomplish his goals. I already told you where to go for more info on self-hypnosis, but here it is again. *http://stevegjones.com/.*

Once you apprehend a new success strategy you take action with your Dynamic Strategic Action Weapon. Ready, Aim, Fire.

Strategic Action

On page 882 of his masterpiece "Human Action" the great praxeologist Ludwig von Mises states *"Whatever the future may have in store for him (man or woman), he cannot withdraw from the necessities of the actual hour. As long as a man lives, he cannot help obeying his cardinal impulse, the élan vital. It is man's innate nature that he seeks to preserve and to strengthen his life, that he is discontented and aims at removing uneasiness, that he is in search of what he may call happiness."*

The Rationally Selfish Individual believes in taking purposeful action to achieve his goals. Action is the name of the game. Strategic Action gets the results you desire. Let's expose some dangerous enemies of action. We'll call the following the "Dozing Dozen" because you might as well be asleep if you allow these to get in your way.

1. I'm not sure what to do.
2. Perhaps I will take care of this soon.
3. This is something I can do in the future.
4. Someday I'll get on this.
5. Tomorrow seems like a good time to work on my DEFINITE PURPOSE in Life.
6. One day, I will get around to this.
7. I going to start my new project next week.
8. In time I'll get started on my goals and desires.
9. I feel like taking it easy, I'll do this later.
10. When are you going to take care of this? Not yet, I have to think on it.
11. I bought you a new motivational book. When are you going to read it? I don't know. Whenever.
12. Damn, I so stressed out I never get anything done.

Once you're confronted by one of these deadly enemies of success, you immediately access your Dynamic Strategic Action Weapon and begin firing away. You might end up taking all twelve out of action.

Procrastination wears many disguises and appears immortal, so expect a lifetime battle of wits. It will constantly tempt you with short-term pleasures. It's doubtful you will win every battle. What do you do if you succumb to its enticing temptations? You access your Dynamic Rational Selfishness Weapon. You quickly use it to TAKE CHARGE of your thoughts, feelings, actions. Remember you not only wield it, you are it. If you forget it, I'm locking you in a room with two dozen irrationally selfish people. All right, I'm just kidding. I don't believe in inhuman punishment. You might use your Dynamic Weapons to permanently obliterate their irrational selfishness. It's questionable whether the poor souls can withstand the continuous assault of the ammo of logic, reason and individualism. Anyway, Social Altruists will accuse you of violating human rights.

When you wake up in the morning, you should know exactly what you will do to accomplish your DEFINITE PURPOSE and your secondary goals. It's also nice to plan your recreational time. Would you believe that an irrationally selfish person could accuse you of living a dull life. They claim winging it makes life more spontaneous.

Well what about spontaneity? Does the irrationally selfish person have a valid point. Retrieve your Dynamic Strategic Action Weapon and eliminate another one of life's illusions. Ready, Aim, Fire continuously. A disorganized, untidy, time-wasting person discourages spontaneity from showing up. A person who creates productive time invites it into his life. Obviously, if you continually struggle to accomplish even minor chores, you won't have any time to be spontaneous. An organized person frees up time to experience the joy of his existence. Your Dynamic Joy of Existence Weapon thrives on time, sweet precious time. Does anyone actually believe that the person who is stressed out from a chaotic environment captures the joy of his or her existence. The idea borders on absurdity. Still, don't expect irrationally selfish people to see through illusion while slumbering their life away.

Here's a quote from Stephen King's "'Salem's Lot The Illustrated Edition" *"At three in the morning the blood runs slow and thick, and slumber is heavy. The soul either sleeps in blessed ignorance of such an hour or gazes about itself in utter despair. There is no middle ground"* Irrationally selfish people experience King's 3AM almost all day and all of the night.

You might not accept Stephen King's philosophy of life, but he certainly writes some powerful verse. I enjoyed his books. Dean Koontz is another master of the horror genre. These gentlemen know how to create a vivid scene that pulls you in. The Rationally Selfish Individual often possesses a wide range of literary interests.

Procrastination relentlessly chases those who fail to pursue their DEFINITE PURPOSE with passion and desire. A burning desire to accomplish your highest values smokes out the master of the stall.

Ayn Rand says *"A desire presupposes the possibility of action to achieve it; action presupposes a goal which is worth achieving."* If you don't have anything to look forward to what's the point of taking action. If you wander around aimlessly, expect reality to disarm you of your Dynamic Rational Selfishness Weapon. Soon you'll be drifting around naked and weaponless.

Your Dynamic Strategic Action Weapon transforms your DEFINITE PURPOSE and your secondary goals and desires into reality. It makes sure you manifest that which you desire. It spells out the way you employ your other Dynamic Weapons to meet your objectives. You take a number of direct actions to achieve your highest values. You succeed.

Conclusion

You captured another Dynamic Weapon. You now have all 8 of your Dynamic Weapons secured in your psychological arsenal of attack and self defense.

1. Anti-Social Altruism
2. Anti-Irrational Selfishness
3. Rational Selfishness
4. Unhampered Capitalism
5. Mind Power
6. Accelerated Awareness
7. Joy of Existence
8. Strategic Action

Robert Meyer

I'm excited to say that I expect to have a high-powered surprise for you, but first I must capture it. Apparently, it's a secret. I just know of its existence. Once it's in my possession, I will reveal it to you. Look forward to Chapter Ten.

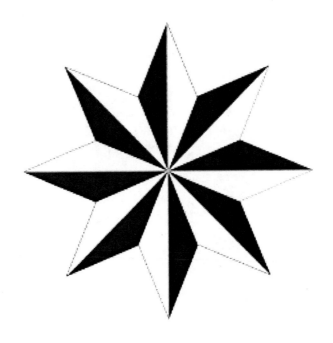

The Rationally Selfish Individual expresses his life as his highest value. He exists to pursue his DEFINITE PURPOSE and to enjoy the pleasures of the body, mind and spirit.

CHAPTER TEN

DYNAMIC SECRET WEAPON AND BEYOND

Good news! I decided to invite you to join me for the search of the Dynamic Secret Weapon. Bring your other Dynamic Weapons with you because you will need them. If you forget your Dynamic Rational Selfishness Weapon you're uninvited. You will go back to the first grade (I remember when my mentor sent me back to the first grade. My first grade teacher Miss Pine threatened to send me back to kindergarten. Anyway, let's not go into that.) and write 101 times on the blackboard, I am the Dynamic Rational Selfishness Weapon. I know. You don't want to be treated liked some irrationally selfish ignoramus. What do you call someone who leaves home naked and unarmed? A complete fool, an irrationally selfish ignoramus. Obviously, that doesn't apply to you.

So far, here's a list of the impeccable warriors who signed up for our journey. Phil, Sophia, Steve, Emma, Olivia, Jackson, Liam, Jessica, Glenn, Brittany, Samantha, Jason, Tyler, Daniel, Justin, Mary, Susan, Lisa, David, Chris, Robert, Marcia, Mark, George, Gail, Brian, Peter, Denise, John, Nathaniel, Dean, Marilyn, Melissa, Jim, Joe, Greg, Toni, Terri, Michael, Pat, Brenda, Buddy, Kenneth, Bill, Troy, Jeanne, Joanne, Frank, Barbara, Arnold, Pamela, Walter, Gloria, Donald, Ernie, **Add your name**. Let's begin our journey.

Cosmic Consciousness

We will begin our search for the Dynamic Secret Weapon by exploring Cosmic Consciousness. Arm yourself with your Dynamic Weapons of Mind Power and Accelerated Awareness.

According to the Wikipedia Encyclopedia in 1901 a Canadian psychiatrist, Richard Maurice Bucke, released his findings in a book titled "Cosmic Consciousness: A Study in the Evolution of the Human Mind." He defined Cosmic Consciousness as a higher form of consciousness than what the ordinary man possesses." Now that sounds like something quite "Dynamic."

Bucke stated that he discerned three forms, or degrees, of consciousness:

1. Simple consciousness, which is possessed by both animals and mankind.
2. Self-consciousness, which is possessed by ordinary men and women, encompassing thought, reason, and imagination. **Note:** Some irrationally selfish people certainly try to refute this statement. However, the logical structure of the human brain is an "a priori" category of human action and remains undeniable.
3. Cosmic Consciousness, which is a higher form of consciousness than that possessed by the ordinary man.

Now that seems rather intriguing. We may be on to something. Let's continue our exploration into Cosmic Consciousness. Make sure you load the two Dynamic Weapons you'll need.

D.J. Moores said *"Bucke's cosmic consciousness is an interconnected way of seeing things "which is more of an intuitive knowing than it is a factual understanding."* I'm sure you can see the problem. Intuitive knowing might help the individual make a decision that's in his best interest, but without facts and a correct theory to back up the facts there is absolutely no proof for an assertion. We do like the idea of seeing the interconnectiveness of concepts and natural phenomena.

Moores also pointed out that for scholars of the purist camp, the experience of cosmic consciousness is incomplete without the element of love, "which is the foundation of mystical consciousness."

As Rationally Selfish Individuals, we're here on earth. If during a meditation we experience universal oneness and a love of "all there is" that's wonderful. If we come out of the experience with compassion and understanding, we gained something of inestimable value. However, we want to use our consciousness to accelerate our growth in everyday life. We love our highest values—and we love and cherish that special person in our life. We're not floating out in the ether like some "space cadet." Our spirit and mind soars while we plant our feet firmly on the ground.

William James understood "cosmic consciousness" to be a collective consciousness, a "larger reservoir of consciousness," which manifests itself in the minds of men and remains intact after the dissolution of the individual. It may "retain traces of the life history of its individual emanation."

That's not encouraging. The Rationally Selfish Individual certainly does not seek his dissolution. That smacks of selflessness. In addition, he uses his Dynamic Anti-Irrational Selfishness Weapon to remove the influence of the second-handedness of the collective (un)consciousness. He doesn't desire to join a crowd of irrationally selfish people. If Williams James is referring to the afterlife it doesn't help us out, although I'm sure his speculations are quite interesting.

Juan A. Herrero Brasas said that Bucke's cosmic consciousness refers to the evolution of the intellect, and not to "the ineffable revelation of hidden truths." According to Brasas, it was William James who equated Bucke's cosmic consciousness with mystical experience or mystical consciousness.

We're all for the the evolution of the intellect and we don't mind discovering hidden truths. Social Altruists would prefer that we didn't uncover any truth or justice. Ineffable means too great or extreme to be expressed or described in words. Sure, we want to feel the ineffable joy of our existence, but the Dynamic Secret Weapon possesses more solidity. Unlike the illusions of Social Altruists, it's not a will-o'-the-wisp. We must move on. Our journey continues.

Exploring Nature

Nature reveals many mysteries. Maybe we will find our Dynamic Secret Weapon concealed in the wonders of nature. Once again you need your Dynamic Weapons of Mind Power and Accelerated Awareness. We will split up and go our separate ways. Each of you can explore a facet of nature that pleases you. You make the choice. When we meet again we will put together our findings. Maybe we will figure out where the Dynamic Secret Weapon is—or maybe someone will find it. Let's get moving.

Several days later. I read your reports and learned quite a bit about the joys of nature. Some of you use your Dynamic Weapons more effectively than I use them. You're surpassing your teacher. What more could I ask for. Here's a synopsis of your experiences.

Individuals succeed in life by overcoming the obstacles nature puts in their path. The creative man and woman transforms nature. It's an illusion to believe we can throw back time and return to the ways of nature. Ludwig von Mises stated *"The natural scarcity of the means of sustenance forces every living being to look upon all other living beings as deadly foes in the struggle for survival, and generates pitiless biological competition."* When we cooperate under the division of labor we transform the survival of the fittest (in a physical sense) into supplying each others need in the marketplace. Social Altruists subvert the beneficial process with their anti-life social schemes. It's time to go for your Dynamic Weapons of Anti-Social Altruism and Unhampered Capitalism. Ready, Aim, Fire. Repeat.

People still enjoy nature in its natural state. Nature hints of romance in its beauty and majesty. Sending your sweetheart flowers always reaches her heart. Wherever you go you find yourself surrounded by plants and flowers. Imagine how empty and desolate a neighborhood would seem if trees weren't lining the streets and standing strong and peaceful in the yards.

You refresh your spirit when you respond to the sighs of nature. Go to a park, hike in the woods or visit an arboretum and immerse yourself in nature. Your body, mind and spirit needs the quietude—the renewal that reinvigorates you, so you can once again accomplish your goals and desires.

Mountain climbing, walking along the beach of an ocean or lake—or sleeping on the desert floor during a cool night can be stimulating.

When I am in nature and one with nature my mind becomes quiet. The pressures and concerns of everyday life melt away. I'm back with my source. I experience the joy of my existence. My creative juices are flowing. I have discovered some of my best ideas during this state of accelerated awareness.

Experiencing oneness with nature allows you to explore your senses. You feel the refreshing breeze that cools you on a warm day or stimulates you on a cool day. As it rustles through the trees—the leaves respond with gentle sounds almost in harmony with your pleasant sighs.

Taking in the fresh breath of nature, you delight in the sensual aroma of flowers and fresh air. You can taste the sweetness of lilac and honeysuckle.

You also delight in the chirping of birds with their musical sounds that transports you into a state of reverie. As they glide through the branches and leaves of the trees they are as ephemeral as an angel passing through your vision.

Strolling deeper in the woods a babbling brook suddenly appears in your path. When your senses of sight and sound experience clear clean water gliding over rocks it's as if the steady flow tenderly caresses your being. You glance upwards and see the sun displaying an array of golden rays through the leaves and branches of the trees.

You happily walk up the path following the lead of a dragonfly. As it floats away you by chance come upon two butterflies participating in the dance of life. They come together—then fly apart—only to crossover and come together again. Flowers sway to a gentle breeze on a colorful, illuminating spring day.

They seem to be giving you a lesson in love and life. Yes, existence is wonderful, a non-repeatable value. The Rationally Selfish Individual expresses his life as his highest value. He exists to pursue his DEFINITE PURPOSE and to enjoy the pleasures of the body, mind and spirit.

You guys and gals are amazing. (Are those terms politically correct? Heck, who cares. We blow that BS away.) You soar in Rational Selfishness. The irrationally selfish person will never experience the sensitivity that impeccable warriors experience.

You know that denying yourself the pleasures of existence is a dreary way to live. It is difficult to understand why anyone would advocate a life of denial and self-sacrifice. Live your life with passion and desire. Life is to be experienced to the utmost. Go for the gusto. Enjoy the fruits of nature. When Social Altruists approach you with their anti-life philosophy of selflessness and self-sacrifice you know what to do. Proudly display your Dynamic Weapons. I think I see the varmints scattering in every direction. What's really cool is that they can't pass gun control laws to take them away from you because your Dynamic

Weapons are psychological.

If irrationally selfish people want to live a life less than it could be that is their privilege—although it's rather sad. Just make sure you diminish the influence they have on your precious life.

We experienced the wonders of nature and learned some valuable lessons but we didn't find the Dynamic Secret Weapon. Still, I wonder about those butterflies. Let's continue our search.

Cause and Effect Relationships

It's been said that *"When a butterfly flaps its wings in one part of the world it can cause a hurricane in another part of the world."* We understand that's probably an exaggeration; however, it points out the fact of cause and effect relationships in the sphere of human action. Maybe, just maybe we're on the track of the Dynamic Secret Weapon.

Causality is one of the "a priori" categories of human action. The Oxford Dictionaries supplies us an excellent definition of "a priori." **Note:** I place the word a priori "a priori" inside quotation marks to avoid confusion.

adjective
Relating to or denoting reasoning or knowledge that proceeds from theoretical deduction rather than from observation or experience.
Adverb
In a way, based on theoretical deduction rather than empirical observation.

In the Dynamic Success Solution book "7 Destructive Economic Illusions Conquered" I explain causality and the other "a priori" categories of human action. *"Cause and effect relationships exist in every action. I'm sure you realize that effective actions raise the possibility of you achieving what you desire. In addition, you know regularity exists in natural phenomena, making it possible for you to plan and act. You certainly couldn't act effectively in a chaotic physical environment."* So you can see it's all practical. You must take correct actions to achieve the desired results.

8 Dynamic Weapons for Conquering Life's Illusions

If you want to achieve your DEFINITE PURPOSE in Life you can't swim in a swamp of contradictions. Let's define the law of non-contradiction? Essentially, "two contradictory propositions cannot both be true at the same time in the same sense." In other words A is A not B.

Social Altruists use the anti-life philosophy of selflessness and self-sacrifice to confuse you into acting in their best interests. These parasites replaced the ironclad law of non-contradiction with Orwellian doublespeak. Take for instance the term selflessness. Honestly, can you have an existence if you don't have yourself. Their scam is so effective that Oxford Dictionaries define selflessness as "Concerned more with the needs and wishes of others than with one's own."

Remember the Seven Principles of the Joy of Existence for the Rationally Selfish Individual to Embrace. The first principle is: Everyone acts in what they believe to be their own best interest. Could self-interest be the Dynamic Secret Weapon? We can conclude it's part of the Dynamic Rational Selfishness Weapon. Rational Selfishness and rational self-interest go hand in hand.

Well, how about the "a priori" category of causality? We recognize cause and effect relationships. We design our Dynamic Weapons with many facets of reality, causality being one of them. Even though we're on the right track, it's not the Dynamic Secret Weapon.

You may wonder what other facets of reality we use to design our Dynamic Weapons. We won't go into great detail, because you can wield them without knowing how they're made. There's always the "a priori" categories of human action.

1. Causality
2. Time
3. Uncertainty
4. Change
5. Logic
6. Value

Does the uncertainty component confuse you? Ludwig von Mises states in "Human Action" *"The uncertainty of the future is already implied in the very notion of acting."* In addition, if your Dynamic

Weapons didn't allow you to adjust for the chaotic conditions Social Altruists spawn, you would completely spin out of balance.

Axiomatic concepts are the foundational building blocks of your Dynamic Weapons.

1. Existence
2. Identity
3. Consciousness

You just discovered another reason why Cosmic Consciousness isn't the Dynamic Secret Weapon we seek.

Without existence, identity and consciousness there would be no Dynamic Weapons and there definitely wouldn't be a you to wield them. You can see why we refer to the Social Altruists philosophy of selflessness and self-sacrifice as anti-life.

Accurate Thought

I believe we methodically close in on the Dynamic Secret Weapon. Let's explore accurate thought. Detective Sergeant Joe Friday of the TV series "Dragnet" was purported to consistently used the catchphrase *"Just the facts, ma'am."* In fact, he never said it. Stan Freberg featured it in his parody of Dragnet. We just conquered another illusion, although that one wasn't really important. The catchphrase supplies us the critical lesson.

Accurate thought requires that instead of "winging it" you get the facts. Next you differentiate between important and unimportant facts. It's similar to implementing your strategy by listing each possible activity A, B, C, D. Obviously, there are A and B facts and unimportant facts.

The Rationally Selfish Individual strives for accuracy in his thinking. Irrationally selfish people often accept gossip, propaganda, half-truths and lies as facts. Social Altruists master doublespeak which is meant to elevate illusions into truth. It makes you wonder how these lyin' thievin' scoundrels can live with themselves. Time to access your psychological arsenal of attack and self-defense. Ready, Aim, Fire, Fire, Fire, Fire, Fire and continue to Fire. Reload when necessary. Say bye, bye to life's illusions. It would be nice if Social Altruists were illusions.

Napoleon Hill says *"You might as well begin to prepare yourself to understand that it requires the staunchest and most unshakable character to become an accurate thinker."* It appears he is describing the Rationally Selfish Individual. We will have no problem closing in on accurate thought.

What does it take to see the facts of reality clearly? Ayn Rand tells us *"Reason, the faculty that perceives, identifies, and integrates the material provided by the senses, does not work automatically. Man is free to think or not to think. The tool of thought is logic – the act of non-contradictory identification."*

Wait a minute. Did we miss something? Could our Secret Dynamic Weapon be Non-Contradiction? Let's see if we can figure it out.

Several of our perceptive students pointed out that non-contradiction actually belongs to the three axiomatic concepts and is an important facet of our Dynamic Weapons.

The Dynamic Secret Weapon

Remember, when I said I still wonder about those butterflies. Trish Phillips writes in Pure Spirit *"For many, the beginning of the New Year signals a sense of transformation – a time to evaluate life in its current state and set goals for manifesting change. The butterfly symbolizes transformation and joy. Its dance reflects the need for movement from where we are to our next phase of being."* I don't need to elaborate on her statement. I see a lot of knowing smiles. We're on the verge of capturing the Dynamic Secret Weapon.

I'm thinking about William Ernest Henley's poem "Invictus" where he ended it with *"I am the master of my fate: I am the captain of my soul."*

Now that's powerful. While incarcerated at Robben Island prison, Nelson Mandela recited the poem to other prisoners and was empowered by its message of self-mastery. Talk about taking advantage of adversity.

Napoleon Hill stated *"You are the "master of your fate" and the "captain of your soul," by reason of the fact that you control your own thoughts, and, with the aid of your thoughts, you may create whatever you desire."* Yes! The Dynamic Secret Weapon is in our possession.

The Rationally Selfish Individual TAKES CHARGE of his thoughts, feelings and actions. Irrationally selfish people seldom do. The Social Altruist discourages it because he thrives on helpless victims. The TAKE CHARGE mentality is much more scarce than the precious metals.

I am proud to state that we just captured the Dynamic TAKE CHARGE Weapon. Really, we had it all along. That's why I referred to the "open sesame" phrase. For strategic purposes we will continue calling it the Dynamic Secret Weapon. Here's a list of our 8 Dynamic Weapons plus 1.

1. Anti-Social Altruism
2. Anti-Irrational Selfishness
3. Rational Selfishness
4. Unhampered Capitalism
5. Mind Power
6. Accelerated Awareness
7. Joy of Existence
8. Strategic Action

And our Dynamic Secret Weapon.

Our psychological arsenal of Dynamic Weapons allows us to conquer the enemies of personal liberty and economic freedom. Let's TAKE CHARGE, get moving and experience the thrill of moving beyond life's illusions.

Is Rational Selfishness for You?

We have traveled a long way, you and I. You learned the virtues of Rational Selfishness. In addition, you possess 8 Dynamic Weapons plus the Dynamic Secret Weapon. There are seven possible responses you could be having to what you read.

1. You are already a Rationally Selfish Individual and you now

possess an psychological arsenal of Dynamic Weapons. You're quite adept at conquering life's illusions. In addition you consistently experience the joy of your existence.
2. You're dedicated to acting from Rational Selfishness and practicing with your Dynamic Weapons. You carefully read each page and captured some practical experience. You're feeling pretty darn good.
3. You finished the book and are now determined to put Rational Selfishness and the teachings into action **ASAP**.
4. You finished the book but you need some time to get your life in order before you can embark on the path of Rational Selfishness.
5. You don't know if Rational Selfishness is right for you. You have your doubts.
6. You think the book is full of it. Rational Selfishness is mean and brutish. The Dynamic Weapons are wrong, anti-social and destructive and you believe I must be in league with Randians, right-wing crazies, anarchists or something to that effect.
7. You are a master of Rational Selfishness and you could teach me a thing or two about wielding the Dynamic Weapons.

If you experienced one of the first three responses then congratulations are in order. So I am going to begin by discussing the fourth response.

Response #4

Have you considered that waiting to first get your life in order is the old proverbial cart before the horse philosophy? The reason your life isn't in order is because you currently are not acting from Rational Selfishness. Putting your Dynamic Weapons into action to conquer life's illusions remains a distant dream.

Nobody's life is perfect. Even a high level of existence has it trials and tribulations—although they appear as higher level problems. **You must begin now.**

Change can be traumatic—so make one change at a time. In the movie "What About Bob" Richard Dreyfuss played Bob's Psychiatrist Dr.

Leo Marvin. Bill Murray starred as the obsessive-compulsive Bob Wiley. Dr. Marvin would advise Bob to take baby steps. One little change at a time. It is like the old question "How do you eat an elephant?" One bite at a time.

An old Chinese saying is *"A journey of a thousand miles begins with a single step."* Begin changing your life today. Do it nice and easy. I guarantee that I didn't capture Rational Selfishness and my Dynamic Weapons in record time. I stumbled around quite a bit. I wrote this book in order to help you avoid some of the unpleasant experiences I suffered during my search for enlightenment. Here are some recommendations that should help you considerably. Remember, you possess the Dynamic Weapons. Use them!

1. If you and your partner haven't experienced the joys of lovemaking recently, set some time aside and do it. If it isn't as enjoyable as you would like, don't worry about it. In the next night or two try it again.
2. Instead of watching television listen to some of your favorite music. One of my favorite places to visit is YouTube.
3. Hug your loved ones and tell them how much you love them. Affection feels good.
4. Carefully watch your thoughts. Every time you have a negative thought change it by thinking of something positive. The Rationally Selfish Individual TAKES CHARGE of his thoughts, feelings and actions.
5. Turn your list of goals into affirmations. Read your goals out loud with emotion at least twice a day. The best times to do this are in the morning before or after you meditate and once again before you go to bed.
6. If you start worrying about your problems breathe in and out slowly a few times and relax. Think about one of your problems as you breathe in and release it as you breathe out. Do this with each problem.
7. If meditation and exercise seem too time consuming or just too hard to do—begin these practices slowly. Start out by meditating five minutes a day—everyday. The same with exercise. Exercise

five minutes a day every other day or three times a week. Then increase it one minute per day. You will be pleased with the results.
8. Read a book that inspires you. New ideas are food for the brain—just as your meals are food for the body. Continuous learning results in your explorations of Rational Selfishness expanding.
9. If you are bored with your meals eat something different. Experiment with different kinds of food.
10. Come up with your own ideas on how you can do things differently. Unleashing your creativity gathers in many rewards.
11. List all the irrationally selfish activities you indulge in and vow to eliminate them from your life. You do possess the Anti-Irrational Selfishness Weapon.

It's time to embark on the most exciting journey of your life.

Response #5

If you aren't sure Rational Selfishness is right for you ask these questions: Is guilt and fear holding you back? Have you adopted a hand me down moral code? Do you believe enjoying the pleasures of the body, mind and spirit is somehow sinful?

And the big question: Are you letting some organization or other people set down a code of living for you—or are you an independent thinker who makes up his own mind about how to live?

You know—you can allow others to dictate how you should live. You can let Social Altruists control your life. Remember this: they aren't you and they will not be the ones who experience your pain and suffering when your life isn't as pleasurable as it could be. In fact, they will probably be extremely pleased because you will be another victim they can "rescue." Arm yourself with your Anti-Social Altruism Weapon now! Ready, Aim, Fire.

Response #6

You think the book is full of it. Rational Selfishness is mean and brutish. The Dynamic Weapons are wrong, anti-social and destructive—and you believe I must be in league with Randians, right-wing crazies, anarchists or something to that effect.

It's obvious you sold your mind, body and spirit to Social Altruists long ago. These purveyors of human misery own you lock, stock and barrel. You must accept their politically correct assertions. You are not allowed ideas of your own. You are imprisoned by life's illusions.

I guess it's your perfect right to believe what you want. If it pleases you write a critique of Rational Selfishness and anything else you don't like about this book. Should you change your mind, the Rationally Selfish Life awaits you.

Response #7

If you are one of those individuals who could teach me a few tricks about experiencing Rational Selfishness—you're a person I want to talk to. You obviously exist as an advanced Master of Life—an impeccable warrior. You have my admiration. I am a willing student if you are generous enough to impart some wisdom to me.

And that's the way—always learning. I learned quite a bit writing this book. Richard Bach stated *"You teach best what you most need to learn."* Be a student of life. Never stop learning. That which you already know may be improved on. I am learning something new every day of my life. I'm grateful to all my teachers—and to the ones that may cross my path in the future.

Before we wrap it up—and it's a gift wrapped with joy, let's clear up any misunderstandings about personal and Social Altruism that might interfere with your endeavors to act from Rational Selfishness.

Altruism – To Give or Not to Give

Many wax on about the virtues of altruism as if this philosophy firmly stands as the "end all" in human relations. They decide it is better to give than receive. Now if they prefer giving to receiving that is their perfect right. In fact giving joyously to another person just plain feels good—especially if it helps someone turn their life around.

However, what we must consider is the disastrous results that tragically arrive when people turn joyous giving into the anti-life philosophy of Social Altruism—enforced by law.

Regard for the Well-Being of Others

Has it occurred to you the Rationally Selfish Individual desires to interact with his fellow humans by trading value for value? In fact, he prefers what Stephen Covey calls a "win-win" relationship.

You already know Social Altruists believe in and viciously attempt to enforce self-sacrifice and self-denial? Time to wield your Dynamic Anti-Social Altruism Weapon. Ready, Aim, Fire

Think about this. The Social Altruist unhappily accomplishes what a an impeccable warrior calls a win-lose exchange or relationship—although the Social Altruist vehemently denies this fact with his penchant for doublespeak.

Illogically, the selfless person gives without receiving anything of value in return. You're probably intelligent enough to know that in practice the one who advocates Social Altruism receives benefits at the expense of others. You see this sorry state of affairs in the political games our leaders play with the hapless citizens.

Consider this controversial fact—although it shouldn't be. The Rationally Selfish Individual respects the natural rights of others. He treats each person as a unique individual he could possibly trade value for value with. He respects an individual's life, liberty and property. He advocates the social system of unhampered capitalism. Yes! We love our Dynamic Unhampered Capitalism Weapon.

You may still doubt the undeniable fact that the Social Altruist treats fellow men and women as a sacrificial victims. He expects them to give and give without receiving anything in return. Since most people prefer not to voluntarily sacrifice their best interests—the Social Altruist enlists the strong arm of government to force these defenseless people to hand over their values. He has no regard for their life, liberty and property. He supports the predatory social systems of socialism and government interventionism. Let's access our psychological arsenal of

Dynamic Weapons.

To Give or Not to Give

Here's the way it is. The "generous" Social Altruists extort value from innocent victims under a social system based on self-sacrifice. It's dishonest and immoral. It's nothing but legalized theft.

Compare the following with the Social Altruist's anti-life philosophy of selflessness and self-sacrifice.

Voluntarily giving to another results in the individual (you) experiencing pleasurable psychological effects. You actually enjoy performing good deeds. If you highly value this person, the effect is one of intense joy. Even performing a favor for a stranger can be rewarding. When you receive the rewards of joy and pleasure, you acquire some of the highest values life has to offer. Of course, you make sure your giving doesn't sabotage your well-being or the person you're helping.

You know it is wise to decide what your most precious values are. You realize that you never purposely trade or sacrifice a higher value for a lower value. Obviously, it is irrationally selfish to do so—and definitely not in your best interest.

You now understand why many people don't experience joy in their giving. They tragically sacrifice higher values for lower values. Unfortunately, their selfless giving actually causes them to become bitter, resentful people. Finally they develop an irrational hatred for the very people they are helping. Have you ever wondered why irrationally selfish people, Social Altruists and government bureaucrats seem so hateful at times?

Giving to others when you aren't sacrificing your highest values—results in you discovering joy and pleasure. You are a Rationally Selfish Individual in your giving.

Here's the bottom line. If you're sacrificing higher values for lower values or for none at all, giving to others is disastrous for all concerned. You have become a Social Altruist who destroys values. You will never experience the supreme joy of your existence.

The solution to finding meaning in your existence is to become a Rationally Selfish Individual. You celebrate the joy of your existence. Aren't you happy that you discovered such a wonderful Dynamic

Weapon? The irrationally selfish person who falls for the anti-life nonsense of a Social Altruist suffers an unrewarding, selfless experience. You've heard *"The road to Hell is paved with good intentions."* If you alternate between Social Altruism and irrational selfishness you travel on the road to Hell.

Conclusion

The Rationally Selfish Individual lives by his or her highest values—whether anyone likes it or not. You exist as an impeccable warrior who possesses unshakable courage. You single-mindedly advance towards your DEFINITE PURPOSE in Life and your secondary goals and desires. You capture the joy of your existence by experiencing the pleasures of the body, mind and spirit. You add icing to the cake by effectively wielding your Dynamic Weapons.

It is time to go. I enjoyed our time together. I found it rewarding and joyous. Maybe somewhere on the path of Rational Selfishness we will meet—and that would be wonderful. Since I have some pleasures of the body, mind and spirit to engage in, I bid you farewell. Uh oh! I just spotted a Social Altruist climbing out of a sewer pipe. Ready, Aim, Fire. Bullseye! Nothing like experiencing the success of my Dynamic Weapons.

I am parting with these words. It is my desire that you experience the joys and ecstasies of Rational Selfishness—and that your Dynamic Weapons defend your personal liberty and economic freedom—always.

It is my desire that you experience the joys and ecstasies of Rational Selfishness—and that your Dynamic Weapons defend your personal liberty and economic freedom—always.

The Author

Robert Meyer was born in Cincinnati, Ohio. He possesses an extensive background in many areas. For 35 years, he has studied economics, philosophy, psychology and metaphysics, integrating these disciplines into a coherent philosophy of life. For more than 25 years, he has indulged in meditation practices to increase his power of reason and to help him reach accelerated states of awareness. His sales career also supplied him a deeper understanding of human nature.

He realizes there are basic principles of Human Action that will help people become successful at achieving their goals and desires. His knowledge that life is to be lived on a physical, emotional, mental and spiritual level allowed him to discover "The Libertarian Way." He lives in Garland, Texas.

He is the author of Dynamic Success Solution's **7 Destructive Economic Illusions Conquered and 7 Powerful Steps for Conquering Life's Illusions.**

For more information visit his blog: **Way of the Libertarian Warrior** and visit his website: **The Libertarian Way.**

CPSIA information can be obtained
at www.ICGtesting.com
Printed in the USA
FFOW03n0308271215
20022FF